# NO EASY ANSWERS

# NO
# EASY
# ANSWERS

*by*
*Philip M. Klutznick*

*Farrar, Straus and Cudahy*
NEW YORK

FIRST PRINTING, 1961

Copyright © 1961 by B'nai B'rith
Library of Congress catalog card number 61–9885
Published simultaneously in Canada by
Ambassador Books, Ltd., Toronto

Manufactured in the United States of America
by H. Wolff
Designed by Robin Fox

To my wife Ethel and to our children—
for their understanding and encouragement

# Introduction

The origin of this book rests in a random thought shared with two companions on a plane hop from Washington to New York. It was in the closing months of my second, and final, term as president of B'nai B'rith. The opportunity to serve as leader of this largest of Jewish organizations, with a history and tradition that begins in the mid-nineteenth century, was a six-year episode for me, intellectually satisfying, crammed with self-instructive experiences in Jewish living.

We were spinning away the hour's flying time reflecting on this— Maurice Bisgyer, the estimable executive vice president of B'nai B'rith; Bernard Simon, its director of public information; and myself.

Jewish life in America, what it is and *why* it is (and so often provoking as many questions as it provides answers), does not hold still for any single or simple definition. But anyone who probes it—and here I mean as participant, not sightseer—is likely to be captured by its many stimulations.

I can testify to that.

During our talk on the plane a wandering, impulsive idea intruded: whether some of the convictions and studied impressions about Jewish community life, distilled from my adventures in it, might make a book.

My companions said yes; even, as I recall, with convincing enthusiasm. So out of that brief chat, followed by many exhausting hours of communicating a jumbled mosaic of ideas and events to paper, came the chapters that follow.

I offer them without posture as a scholar or savant. In saying this, I suspect I am repeating the conversation of the Jew and the hunchback: the Jew who whispered confidentially, "I must let you in on a secret—I am a Jew"; to which the other responded, "One confidence deserves another—I am a hunchback."

Thus, these pages carry the notions and sensitivities of a layman. What I have learned of Jewish community life, whether it is a maxim to be discarded or clung to, is largely one man's experiences reinforced by the intimacy that comes with varying degrees of leadership in Jewish affairs. I was cast into its whirlpool—really I jumped—as a young man; I owned a membership card in the B'nai B'rith movement before I was old enough to own a razor. A generation of paddling in the swirling waters of Jewish activity (more than once I found myself trying to make it upstream) was intensified by the six exciting years in the presidency of B'nai B'rith. From that vantage and others I sought out my fellow Jews in many places, crisscrossing this continent, traveling to Latin America, to Europe and North Africa and, of course, to Israel. If the airline stubs that bear the legend "P. Klutznick" were heaped together, they could confirm the universality and the durability of Jewish life.

There is no pretense here at autobiography. Whereas parts of the content are narrative and personalized, the intent is to explore some facets of Jewish community life which have a bearing on its future in this country.

A word about the way this book took shape—and I suppose "intermittently" would be the word. The pressures of a full and constant schedule of activities for myself and others who helped in the task created inevitable lapses and delays in the writing and editing chores. Moreover, I learned painfully that the process of assembling material in some kind of orderly process for publication is no casual accomplishment.

In the formative stages, fortified with a reasonably good memory and a dictating machine, I spent several weeks pouring words into the instrument. When the first of these transcribed notes reached Bernie Simon (who had joined me in Park Forest for the birth pangs) they suggested a book twice the content of this shortened venture. But in the meanwhile, the opportunity was afforded me by President Kennedy to serve under Ambassador Adlai Stevenson as a member of the United States Mission to the United Nations. Understandably, in the refinement process, the details of many incidents and the attitudes and actions of many personalities, all of which some day need to be recorded as part of the history of the times, remain, for this book, in the shadows. This is not the time and this is not the book for it.

I might as well confess that this is the second book I have essayed. The first, happily unpublished, was attempted fifteen years ago. I had spent five years in Government, directing a feverish-paced public housing program during wartime. When the assignment ended I felt an urge to write on the nation's housing problems. I collected much material and completed most of the manuscript. But the period between 1945 and 1947 wrought so many changes in our national economy that what I thought important for housing in 1945 was hopelessly outdated in 1947. Any thought of publishing the manuscript was abandoned.

All of which is a reminder that the published word can, at times, be treacherous. Perhaps some of the views and theories set down here with some sense of finality will, in short order, evaporate in the shifting scene, just as some earlier beliefs of mine have been drastically modified by experience.

Nonetheless, what is set down here is written with strong conviction. It is not unlikely that in some areas of discussion I have—to employ playwright Gore Vidal's happy phrase—"treated the obvious as if it had just been discovered." And what I have to say may not resolve any of the myriad problems of an expanding American Jewish life. Finally, there are many persons active and wise in

Jewish affairs who will disagree sharply with the opinions of the author.

All of this, I feel, does not negate my fundamental aspiration for this book: to get more American Jews to think more deeply about American Jewish life; if possible, to get them to differ and debate some of the questions raised in these chapters.

I would like to see the understanding develop that there are many problems in Jewish life and no easy answers to most of them.

One of the weaknesses of the voluntary Jewish community is the mortality rate among those who aspire to leadership in it. They quit early. Many of them do so, I believe, out of a mistaken impression that the road is easy. The true nature of the voluntary society, the stubbornness, apathy and contrariness of the human beings who comprise it, frustrates and disillusions some of our best talent for prospective leadership. A simple awareness of the complex character of Jewish life could dissipate this trend and preserve the talent.

Without the persistent two-way proddings between Bernie Simon and myself it is likely this book would not have been completed. I gratefully acknowledge his participation in all phases of the project. He contributed his editorial talents not as a professional writer or member of the B'nai B'rith staff, but as the good friend I hold him to be.

I have already noted the role of Maurice Bisgyer. I owe him much more than words can convey as my close and knowledgeable colleague during my tenure as president of B'nai B'rith.

In the final stages of this book I called on an able critic, thinker and writer, Sidney Wallach, whose advice and assistance were valuable. I am also indebted to Mrs. Evelyn Greenberg of the B'nai B'rith staff for her assistance in research and checking data when memory failed me, and to publisher John Farrar for his patience, wisdom and encouragement.

PHILIP M. KLUTZNICK

*Park Forest, Illinois*
*January 20, 1961*

NO EASY ANSWERS

# (1)

# *The Cup is Half-Full*

I'm not the steadiest disciple of ritual. So my credentials for believing in formal religion might be open to question. Yet I believe wholeheartedly that without religion Jewish life loses its perpetuating identity. I say this not as a casual expression of sentiment or tradition. The primacy of religion, with its organized institutions and rituals, is fundamental to the term "Jew" and to a continuing American Jewish community.

Jews are, first and enduringly, a *religious* community. This may be challenged by Jewish traditionalists who say Jews are not but *should be* and by Jewish secularists who say Jews *do not have to be*. I might agree with either if they could bolster their view with a simple yet inclusive definition of what, fundamentally, Jews are made of. The more this is wrangled over the stronger emerges the historical evidence that underneath it all we Jews are made of a *religion*. To this may be added—or omitted—any number of ethnic, political or cultural definitions satisfying to the historian or social scientist—or even to the sentimentalist. But subtract religion from Jewish peoplehood and you remove the heartbeat.

I once debated this with a man who was both rabbi and scholar. He disagreed. "I wish it were true that Jews could not exist without religion," he said, "but it isn't so. Look how many Jews are non-observant." He proposed instead a revision of my definition. "What you really mean is that Jews share a common core of Jewish values."

But no, I do not mean that at all. If I did, then Jews could maintain these "values," and comfortably so, as Quakers or as Unitarians, Universalists or Ethical Culturists, and thereby close the book on Jewishness and its special status. For it is at once Judaism's glory and disadvantage that the essential verities that derive from it—monotheism, aspiration for social justice, and ideals of love, morality, and devotion to study—are no longer its exclusive concepts. Their acceptance is widespread, even universal. One does not have to persist as a Jew to preserve these ethical values for himself. The *form* of their expression is another matter.

Is the bond, then, one of a common philosophy? Yet, as I see all around me, the philosophies of Jews throughout the world range in a 360-degree circle and neither the Zionist, the Yiddishist, the social democrat Bundist nor the Jewish theocrat can claim for his philosophy an unbroken link that makes of Jews, everywhere and through the ages, a people. Even the religion of the Jews reveals various and at times startlingly different images.

Yet there is and there always has been *a* centrality to Jewish life, a single cohesive force—its religious character.

When the secularist rebels at this he is quarreling not with the principle but with his indifference to it. Otherwise, why hold himself out as a Jew? What is the common group denominator between the third generation secularist Jew, whose link with his pious great-grandfather has long been cut, and the sabra of Israel, the black-skinned Falasha of Ethiopia, the Jew of Soviet Russia, the anti-

Zionist in Texas and the pious Talmudist transplanted from Poland to a *chassidic* enclave in the Williamsburg neighborhood of Brooklyn, New York? Not nationalism, race, language, politics, ideology, or ethnic culture. It is religion.

That religion is the essence—and here I offer no simple formula or quick, capsule creed of what constitutes Judaism—is something I have learned slowly; not as a youngster in *cheder* but in the process of my own maturing as a Jew searching out the meaning of a Jewish life in a free America. Thirty years of active adult participation in the infinitely varied expressions of this life have imposed this conviction.

It is, I think, a glib and only partially valid appraisal to hold that Jews, especially those who are secular-minded, remain Jews because of gentile pressure. In our voluntary American society, the road to assimilation is open and even comfortable for those who can travel it with conviction. It is still easier for their children. Yet the great mass of American Jewry, no matter how passive in its religious behavior—and is it more so than that of the average, urbanized Protestant?—remains Jewish, unyielding to all the pressures. It was equally so in eras and lands of enforced ghettoization where the external pressures of the gentile community did help to catalyze a flourishing, completely sustaining, though insulated, Jewish life. But the ghetto was something more than gentile prejudice; it also expressed gentile exasperation with Jewish resistance to conversion.

What is it that Jews cling to? Rabbis affiliated with the Mizrachi, the organization of religious Zionists, and those of the anti-Zionist American Council of Judaism may have answers that seem poles apart. Yet each will speak in his own vocabulary of the religious centrality of Jewish existence. We may try to inventory and assign to separate compartments Jewish coherence by other generic phrases: group loyalty, enduring tradition, a common memory of thousands of years of triumphs and tragedies, a sense of mutual destiny. Yet all of the loyalties, traditions, memories, and idea associations have one constant—an identification, however vestigial, of religious faith. One enduring thread, however thin, runs through all of the real or only apparent differences.

Jews, whether pious, indifferent, or rebellious to their religion, nevertheless remain Jews because of that religion. Just as among many non-churchgoing Protestants, the basic identity remains, manifesting itself at the very least in important individual and family events and crises. If there is a house of prayer Jews do *not* go to, they know it is a *shul*.

To identify one's self as Jew is not an experience in a social vacuum. It requires a community that cannot be Jewish without its religious flavor. And every religion needs its *formalities* for its expression: in our case, the synagogue and the emotional elements of its forms and rituals that give it character as an institution.

I differ from the traditionalist and from the insistently protesting secularist because each arrogates Jewishness, or what he deems its essence, to himself. I include them both, along with all others who declare themselves as Jews. Long ago I accepted the universal image of Mordecai Kaplan's thesis of Judaism as a civilization because it appeared to me to be the most suitable image, providing room for everyone—the extremists of Orthodoxy and Reform, the in-between believer, even the non-believer—who is born and remains a Jew. This kind of comprehensiveness is responsive to the realities of the American Jewish community. And while it maintains that Judaism as a civilization is something more than religious dogma and practice, it does not displace the primacy of religion in Jewish life. Instead, it offers the concept of a civilization *predicated on a religious base*.

Of course, civilizations exist without religion. But a Jewish civilization cannot. Otherwise, it might well have hardened into Toynbee's unhappy symbol of a "fossil." It has not done so because the Jewish religion has both its fixed compass points and its free-wheeling interpretations and adjustments to changes in life and society, adjustments that provide equally for the Jews of the Talmudic period, the Jews of the East European *shtetl,* and the Jews of the United States.

That is why the forms and expressions of Judaism—group worship in the synagogue, the study of the Bible, the Sabbath kiddush, the religious school, the solemnity of Yom Kippur, the gaiety of

Hanukah, the *chupa* marriage ceremony—have a primary place, at least in my vision, in the Jewish way of life.

## 2.

Lately it has become fashionable to debate at length the character of what is generally regarded as a religious revival. Is it meaningful or superficial? The outward signs are clear: in the up-surge in congregational membership, in new temple construction, in an expanding Hebrew school enrollment, in other ways. Yet many take a skeptical view, dismissing these developments as no more than a transitory expression of a craving for Jewish identity, a determination to belong. What is lacking, they point out testily, are the commitments to the teachings of Torah and Talmud, of prophets and sages, and to genuine religious spirituality.

The critics are clearly right when they point out that many who provide generous gifts to the building of synagogues neglect to come and to bring their families to worship in those very synagogues. They justly decry the fact that the terminal point for the average Jewish youngster is fixed in teen-age by the Bar Mitzvah rite.

But when they follow these acid observations with jeremiads of doom for Jewish life in America, they are, I think, wrong.

American Jewry is not tumbling into a religious decline. The widespread contemporary affiliation with the synagogue, perhaps greater than at any other time in American Jewish history, has its own meaning and its own potential. It represents a new pattern, a radical departure from the way Jewish religious life was expressed in the Eastern European communities that have now been erased by the Nazi brutality. Our contemporary American Judaism is an instinctive expression by the native-born children of the immigrant from Europe, and of the free environment they discovered here and took to their hearts. In terms of the calendar, it is barely some three generations old. The many advance obituaries, the gloomy prediction of a disintegration of Jewish life in America, make me shake my head in amazement. For as I see it, many of the calamity-howlers relate a distinctive Jewish identity to some form of imposed or voluntary ghetto. And I am led to wonder what it was that the ghetto had that we need and do not have.

The ghetto had anti-Semitism and fear. It had poverty. It had, seen through twentieth-century eyes, an abundance of superstition. It had a crushing timidity that weighed heavily on a burdened and insecure people. It had persecution and despair. To all of these elements the Judaism of its time reacted by nourishing its vital spark within the framework of a separatist ghetto and synagogue life. Then, we are told that as the ghetto walls, maintained for a while even in this country by a first generation of immigrants determined to sustain their familiar patterns of life, crumbled under the liberated onrush of a native-born American generation, the synagogue and Jewish religion lost their physical dominance and even meaning and that the Jewish residue, for all of its ancient traditions and cultural values, seemed to yield its flavor to the alien herbs of a melting pot.

Does this mean that Jewish life, in order to survive, needs the adversity, parochialism, and discipline of the ghetto?

It does not. It means only that the "lost generation" of American Jews, the youngsters of the pre-1930's who broke away from the synagogue, who hid their prayer shawls, changed their names, and dabbled in a militant humanism, apparently removed from their religious origins, for a while knew no better and came to the superficial conclusion that they had nowhere to go as Jews.

The romanticists who self-indulgently probed this period have called it, out of their tormented nostalgia, a mass form of Jewish "self-hatred." This is a colorful theory by which you can write endless articles of lamentation or plot seamy novels of life on New York's East Side.

It is, however, also careless reasoning. For the young Jews to whom it refers were not hating themselves as Jews but rejecting the anachronistic character of the Jewishness that surrounded them at the time and which had not as yet made its inevitable American adjustment. There was as yet no American idiom that would embrace their Jewish identity. They saw only a Hobson's choice of continuing the alien social façade of the religious forms and expressions brought by their parents along with immigrant baggage. And this they rejected.

It is one of the remarkable properties of Judaism that, phoenix-like, it seems to die and to be reborn. Our "lost" generation, when the final accounting came, did not lose itself in assimilation. It groped its way through a period of defiance and irresolution. It awoke to the meaning of the Hitlerist phenomenon, came to grips with its eternal challenge, and encouraged a new Jewish life-form that was at home in the freedom, mobility, and variety of American life.

The same youngsters who fled the Judaism that reeked of the ghetto are now a generation of parents who want Jewish identity for themselves, who are joining Jewish organizations, building the new temples, and crowding their children into the Jewish religious schools. Some of them have even discovered their long-forgotten *talesim*.

In doing this, the young postwar families of a reawakened Jewry are not isolating themselves, or running against the tide of American community life. They are, as a matter of fact, conforming to the prevalent reality of the United States as essentially a religious-minded if not overtly a religious-practicing nation. Will Herberg rightly points out that the "melting pot" did not really synthesize the varied ethnic cultures of our society into an American amalgam. Its effect was rather to fit the newcomer into a dominant Anglo-Saxon matrix and to submerge the many elements that made him "different." All except one: the immigrant's religious faith. Thus, says Herberg, religion becomes "the differentiating element and the context of self-identification and social location" having permanency in American society. There is a dominant Judaeo-Christian character to American life that does not allow our society completely to forget or dispense with the formal expressions of religion.

Least representative of this reality are the larger metropolitan centers. They are jungles of anonymity where Jew, Protestant, or Catholic can, to all intents and purposes, lose himself completely. In New York City, Jewish identity is formidable by the weight of its population alone. In suburbia, to which Jews have been drawn in an accelerating migration, the need to conform to the general pattern stands out as vividly as the modern glassy architecture of its synagogues. The Jewish family formerly from Brooklyn, where it rarely entered through temple or synagogue doors, has become a more dependable regular at Sabbath services and absorbed in the men's club and sisterhood as well—now that it lives in Rockville Centre.

From the first moment my partners and I stepped to the drawing board for our plans of the community we meant to build at Park Forest, Illinois, we laid out space for churches and synagogues no less than for streets, schools, and utilities. We were not being missionaries or making deferential, if remote, gestures to public relations. We were simply expressing the community developer's awareness of one of the basic conventions of American suburbia. Park Forest had its organized church groups before it had a village government and before most of its streets were paved. The first Jewish newcomers shared the experience of "a *minyan* in someone's living room." And Jewish identity asserted itself in the first year when a B'nai B'rith lodge and women's chapter, and chapters of Hadassah and the National Council of Jewish Women were added to the scene.

The Jewish families who came to Park Forest were in the main refugees from the city—young, energetic, and civic-minded, long on enthusiasm and short on money in the bank. For most, religion had earlier been a taken-for-granted (and therefore a mostly-left-alone) relationship, clinging by a vague nostalgia to a variant of the Orthodoxy of their immigrant parents. But they respected the mores of suburbia; to be part of the community in a real sense meant identifying clearly—even conspicuously—with their religion. "Especially for the children!" the young mothers would say. "They need to learn something about Judaism. Who will prepare the boys for Bar Mitzvah?"

Park Forest was built from scratch on vacant farmland. Its budding Jewish community had to start from scratch, too—

there were no *shuls* or *melamedim* left over from an earlier generation. The young parents had to mortgage themselves with more responsibilities and dig further into their cautiously-budgeted salaries to finance a combined synagogue-temple with religious school facilities.

There were glum voices of despair that these young Jewish families were not struggling to study Torah but only to identify themselves as Jews in their community. Yet surely this was no demonstration of Jews rushing to their religious extinction.

The example of Park Forest is not unique. It appears in suburbia throughout the country. So much so, that its force has swept into the metropolitan centers as well.

### But is it religion?

Long-faced critics ask the question and presume that the obvious answer is the only answer. They deplore it as secularism; they decry it as a "checkbook Judaism." Where is the moral fervor? they ask. Where the love of study? Where the intellectual grappling with a religious philosophy historically so rich in stimulating wisdom?

And they answer: Not in the magnificent new temples that fill up only for High Holy Days services . . . nor in classrooms abandoned by thirteen-year-old students with the equivalent of a fourth-grade religious education. Not in unread books of a rich Jewish literature nor in an unfamiliar Hebrew language.

Among American Jews the cup of religion indeed runneth not over. But it is not, as the critics say, half-empty. The cup is really half-full.

This is not an uncommon episode in Jewish history. By the Biblical account, the children of Israel wandered for two generations, lamenting their exodus from fleshpotted Egypt and bowing to man-made idols, before they reached the Promised Land. The Alexandrian age of Judaism flowered out of its own Hellenistic environment. The remarkable era of Jewish achievement that began in tenth-century Spain (an outgrowth of the Moorish toleration that gave Jews freedom and mobility) was more than five centuries emerging after the decline of the Babylonian era had set in. The whole sweep of Judaism can be told in such historical flows, ebbs, and transitions.

So it may well be in America midway in the twentieth century. We find a new Jewish way of life making its modest way in a free society. It responds to the immutable Jewish urge for self-identity and creativity. It conforms to the religious character of its environment. And, still in its infancy, it is reaching out for its own distinctive qualities.

In this perspective, it is not "checkbook Judaism" we are witnessing, something to be deprecated or dismissed with ridicule. It is a firm step to an American-developed expression of Jewish continuity, the promise of a creatively rich Judaism, part of a multi-millennial history.

I am not excusing the "Yom Kippur Jew" for his desultory piety. But it is also a fact of Jewish life that many a congregation keeps its budget in balance by the contributions it raises Kol Nidre night among those to whom reverence is expressed by this seasonal visitation. The Yom Kippur Jew may be lax in his faith, religiously illiterate; yet he too makes his obeisance, if you will, toward his Jewish self-identity. It is, in its own way, his deed of *Tzedakah:* with what propriety is it scoffed? It is, I know, simplifying; it is also true that the Yom Kippur Jew, however indifferent to the scholarship, the culture, and the worship of Judaism, is nonetheless not the stuff assimilation is made of.

True, this minimal, low-effort Jewish identity is not enough. But why is it deplored as a rejection of Judaism when, plainly, it is a step to affirmation, however inadequate? Without it, how will present-day scholars and sages restore the Jewish spirit to its fuller expression?

Here, then, is the character and problem of religion for American Jewry; an evolutionary form, not of death, but of rebirth. The great need is to encourage and advance this prospect in contemporary satisfying terms. For just as the American nation is itself a new concept in a new environment, so are its mores—religion among them—derivatives from the past for a new, still-emerging society.

3.

It is for the learned theologians to ponder the character and change in the religious structure of American Jewry. I make no plea for change for the mere sake of change; neither can I agree that change, of itself, is a fatal heresy.

My father-in-law, of sainted memory, a Yeshiva bocher in the old country, a successful businessman in his adopted America, never departed from the rules of Orthodoxy. He attended *shul* morning and evening. He shut down his extensive business operations on the Sabbath. He recited the prescribed prayers as he washed his hands or heard the thunder or prepared for a night's sleep. He did all this not in a *chassidic* enclave where it might be commonplace, but in the Midwest's Omaha, where it was not.

His children did not follow in his Orthodox footsteps. They participated in establishing a Conservative congregation. When that happened he reached for his checkbook to make a substantial contribution to the new congregation. "For myself," he said, with, in my judgment, far-seeing wisdom, "I neither want nor need any Conservative amendments to my faith. For my children it may be the answer to keeping them Jewish."

He would not, however, have been patient with today's disruptive squabbling of our denominationalized rabbinate. We find Orthodox, Conservative, and Reform competing vigorously (sometimes intolerantly) for the loyalties of American Jewry. The contentions of one group of rabbis that another is unqualified for rabbinical functions; the disputes as to liturgy publicly argued with irreverent rancor; a handful of Orthodox creedists demanding the excommunication of some Reform brethren—*these schismatic antagonisms are at once painful and perplexing to a Jewish community that is still groping for the fundamentals of religious life.*

I am not suggesting that rabbis submerge or compromise where their differences are compelling. It is their role to challenge error, even among themselves. But this cannot be turned into justification for endless contentiousness. To challenge error in others calls for the admission that error is universal—and human—and as likely to seize one man as another. This perplexed layman wonders: are not the rabbis and religious scholars who pursue factionalism more fervently than they exalt the common qualities of Judaism committing a graver error—that of frustrating a Jewishness in America that is striving for maturity?

The indictment is not directed exclusively against segments of the Orthodox group. Sharp, exclusory denominationalism has its advocates in each of the three major divisions of American Judaism. Sketchily defined, the Orthodox, calling themselves traditionalists, stress Torah as God's clear and immutable revelation of truth and moral law of a divine origin that prohibits amendment or modification (except perhaps by such awesome competence as a Sanhedrin). The Reform, calling themselves liberals, have abandoned revelation and belief in miracles while acknowledging divine inspiration in the human experience of perceiving truth and thereby striving to apply this guidance to life and its changing human institutions. The Conservative (middle-of-the-roaders) defer to both positions and derive their own flexible course; its adherents may abide by the principle of divine revelation at Sinai, or accept it with modification, or reject it in favor of a naturalistic theory, while still others try to synthesize all these concepts.

The confusion of the layman grows as he finds pronounced doctrinal variants within the loose bonds of a single denomination. There is a range—broad and colorful as the spectrum—between old-time, rabbinic traditionalists and modernists in the Orthodox structure; another covering the expanse from classical to moderate Reform; and still another in Conservatism, with, depending on your viewpoint, either its lack of self-definition or a multiplicity of definitions. Which of these is to be the faith of and for the modern Jew?

One conclusion seems clear. If, as some of the rabbinate maintain, a religious revival is needed to rescue the American Jew from the abyss of secularism, it will not be forthcoming out of a welter of confusions, rivalries, and hostilities among the theologians themselves.

Yet, for all that their divergences set the denominations apart, we need to take a second look: Each group accepts the omniscience and eternity of God; each adheres to a distinctively Judaic concept of moral law with its emphasis on and special expression of ethical behavior, love, and social justice; each respects learning and tradition; each follows a recognizably similar form of group worship and ritual; each is imbued with a sense of Jewish history. The significant truth is that the theological concepts that divide Judaism are far less meaningful than the living realities by which Jews are united in a common faith. The Jewish community will, it seems to me, best be served by its religious leaders against the background of these prevailing realities. Certainly the trend toward a revived Judaism can be accelerated only as the emphasis is placed on what unites rather than on what separates Jews.

This does not mean a compulsive unity of religion; no more than does any other form of voluntary association. It does mean, however, that religious leadership needs to accept a mandate for an emphasis on and search for common areas of agreement and cooperation as a means of strengthening the religion of Jews.

What I have here indicated is no general indictment. Most rabbis are realistic souls, immersed in a conscientious calling, recognizing the primacy of their task of teaching Jews to live by Jewish values, happy when by example and preachment they have encouraged a greater awareness of and responsiveness to the eternal verities of Judaism.

Moreover, for all the scholarly thunder, rabbis are often less separated by ideological beliefs than by their loyalties to rabbinical or denominational organizations. This perhaps explains a curious disobedience some of them hold for Jewish sectarianism. Increasingly, many rabbis, in their understandable concern for a hospitable pulpit, move readily from one denomination to the next (or between a denomination's subgroups). For its part, the less doctrinal laity enters upon its religious affiliation with little concern for the niceties of creed or dogma. The synagogue's geographical proximity, the accessibility of its religious school for children, the quality of its physical property, the personality of the rabbi, the cost of its membership dues—these are the more compelling influences.

As with most internal controversies, the denominational struggle in religious Jewry is not a community dispute but a contest of minute elements of its leadership among the competitive, organized religious establishments. In a way, the competition is also a reflection of the increment in strength that has come to all the denominational institutions. Orthodoxy is no longer withering away as an appendix of an Old World cultural pattern such as I knew it in my youth. In its new look it seems to have found more receptivity among native-born American Jews than ever before. The Reform movement, challenged fifty years ago as no more than an erring cult of Jews gone astray for creature comfort, is now enriched with traditionalism; and its congregants increase. Conservatism has flourished by traveling a wide-embracing middle road.

Some striking paradoxes have resulted from the dissensions. The stronger the denominations grow, the more they resemble one another.

So much so that it is at times difficult to distinguish between a Conservative and a modern Orthodox service. At Reform services, a *yarmalke* is at times an accepted custom. The resemblances grow apace.

As to my personal attitudes, I am as pleased as not to worship with my head covered; while, given the choice, I prefer to have my wife and daughter seated with, not apart from, my sons and me. I am deeply moved by a cantor and choir chanting the hymns of the liturgy, but I do not want them to dominate the service and make of the congregation passive observers rather than participants. I am mindful of the use of English to make the service better understood, but I am partial to and affected by the mystic beauty of Hebrew as the language, spanning time and space, of the synagogue. These, assuredly, are idiosyncrasies of my environments, past and present. By official standards of compartmentalized Judaism they are perhaps in conflict with one another. But I am not the only Jew given to a personal eclecticism of tradition and liberalism to fit his own concept of desirable ritual. Truth to tell, except for the extremes of fundamentalist Orthodoxy or classical Reform, I am as comfortable in one synagogue as in the next.

I know I am not qualified to judge the validity of the old and newly emerging varieties of Judaism. There are, however, some economic truths that I do know and that I believe worth considering.

It takes a great deal of money to start a congregation and keep it going and to build and equip a synagogue and its related religious school. The capital and operating fund of most new congregations—and there will be many more Jewish families when the war babies begin marrying in this decade—will have to come largely from the younger element among Jews, those increasingly settling in suburbia, earning $7,500 a year, and struggling with mortgages while rearing, happily but expensively, more children than their parents did. What are they to do? Split their limited resources and build three separate congregations for the sake of distinctions that are, at best, intangible and incomprehensible for them?

Some smaller communities have tried to provide the threefold variety. Perhaps the most obvious defect has shown up in the consequent poor quality of religious schooling—there are neither enough trained teachers to fill the classrooms of three competing synagogue schools nor congregational memberships affluent enough to attract good educators with decent pay.

It is unlikely that American Jewry in the near future will develop an indigenous, synthesized religious movement for all but the few inevitable dissidents. Yet there may be a purpose to exploring a "united synagogue" in at least its physical aspects.

Protestants have experimented with it successfully. Their United Protestant Church movement has flourished in the postwar era, specifically in the burgeoning suburbs where two or three denominational churches cannot meet the community's broader, religiously varied needs. The united church, embracing communicants of a dozen or more denominations in a single congregation, guided by a clergyman who is neither unmindful of, nor overzealous with, denominational distinctions, is serving an economic (and unifying) purpose among Protestants. This experience might with modifications work well for the coming generation of Jews.

How? is the challenging reaction of those who foresee denominational obstacles. This proponent candidly says: "I don't know. But let's try it and see what happens."

It would necessarily begin in the form of individual experiments in suburbia and its developments would depend on local characteristics.

Two factors are impressively in favor of making such an effort. The first is a state of mind—the encouraging attitude which recognizes that religious sectarianism in Jewish life is both an obstacle and a challenge, and that both invite a responsive reaction. An experimental proposal, by its inherent nature, cannot be confined into an incontrovertible blueprint that would renounce the values of trial-and-error experience. David Ben-Gurion's advice is applicable to this subject. "First," he said, "define your objective; declare your need; say what you want. Then, and only then, consider the obstacles. But even then the obstacles must be subordinated to the objective. Never must the objective be renounced in favor of the obstacles."

A second factor is the compelling knowledge that wherever necessity has imposed a counterforce to denominationalism, the results have been good. This is another of the paradoxes. The experience of the Jewish chaplaincy for the American armed forces, for example, makes it evident that where conditions forbid American Jewry to indulge in religious divisiveness the spirit of k'lal Yisroel transcends the differences. If it can work of necessity, why not by reasoned choice?

Not unlike the chaplaincy is the B'nai B'rith Hillel Foundation where students have as pastor a rabbi whose Orthodox, Conservative, or Reform background is sublimated by the overriding concern for a broad spiritual Jewishness of boys and girls on the campus. Here again, the single denominator is k'lal Yisroel. Whatever the degree of success of the Hillel movement in encouraging an affirmative Jewishness among college students, it could not have been achieved if the rabbinical staff allowed itself to be motivated by narrow loyalties.

Rabbi Maurice Pekarsky, a campus rabbi for more than a quarter of a century, put it well: "The Hillel movement, having for all practical purposes transcended the three branches of Judaism, is the only institution or meeting place where Jews of all denominations can gather in an organized fashion and religion *is not* officially excluded."

Another foreseeable value of a "united synagogue" plan is that it could conserve rabbis. Competent rabbis are always in short supply. The call upon a rabbi is not only to man the pulpit. Rabbis are in demand as chaplains, as administrators in Jewish organizational life, as teachers, as youth guidance workers. The Hillel Foundation which has the largest rabbinical staff in the world, is rarely without an imminent vacancy in its ranks.

As Jewish affiliations expand, the competition for qualified rabbis will quicken. The existing seminaries, lacking the physical capacity and understandably unwilling to adopt crash programs in expansion, offer no promise of graduating sufficient numbers into the rabbinate. The shortage will get worse before it gets better.

Training a rabbi involves a substantial community investment. It would seem sensible to make every effort to conserve his usefulness and not to wear him down with denominational schisms. Is it, then, unthinkable to suggest that a rabbinate of surpassing loyalties, with a Reform rabbi able to step into a Conservative pulpit and vice versa, would best serve the totality of Judaism? I know of Yeshiva graduates who are now preaching in Conservative synagogues and Reform temples . . . and for all my earnest efforts I cannot find much fundamental difference between the graduates of the Hebrew Union College-Jewish Institute of Religion, which trains Reform rabbis, and those of the Conservative group's Theological Seminary.

An interchangeable pulpit may be a radical idea. But is it really stranger to the average American Jew than is a factionalized rabbinate?

### 4.

I think, too, that if we are going to conserve our rabbis we ought to stop making of them what they are not.

They are not—and ought not be turned to as—psychiatrists,

investment counselors, political scientists, public relations advisers, drama coaches, or experts on wheat parity.

The rabbi is, or should be, a religious specialist. In the emancipated character of American Jewish life the rabbinical role has lost the monolithic authoritarianism that was its strength four and five decades ago in an immigrant-dominated American Jewry.

What place now for the rabbi in modern Judaism?

The rabbinate itself does not have a clear answer to the question. It has been groping for a status that can integrate much of the tradition of rabbinic authority with the realities of today's communal voluntarism and dispersion. The effort has led to all sorts of compromises for the individual rabbi. The effect for the community has been to miscast the rabbi as a jack-of-all-services.

A newly-ordained rabbi, twenty-five years old and fresh from the seminary, acquires his first pulpit. What does the congregation want of him? Not alone to attend to his ritual and pastoral duties but to do a bit of fund-raising; to be host and socialite; to join the local Rotary; to serve on an unmanageable variety of boards and committees; to organize whatever needs organizing; to be the Jewish stand-in at civic affairs; and generally to become an *all-purpose* community leader overnight.

The young rabbi, unequipped for anything more than his new and still formidable task of being the religious leader, becomes the most over-assigned Jew in town. Little time is left for his traditional commitment as a religious force or as scholar and teacher.

The newcomer to a community who is going to sell insurance or manage the supermarket has to demonstrate leadership qualities before he is elevated to the top levels of a community's councils. Not so the rabbi—who is placed there at once. Of course, I do not equate the average insurance man with the rabbi in leadership capacities; by virtue of his ordination the rabbi is, presumably at least, trained for leadership. His training, however, is that of a *religious* leader, a specialty which does not necessarily embrace the talents of an administrator of a welfare fund or lecturer in political subjects. Why, then, press the rabbi into activities peripheral to his trained calling and in the process misuse his genuine talents for congregational activities? Is this not an aberration for which the community itself is to blame? Should we be surprised when he is found wanting—in the profusion of responsibilities flung upon him or eagerly volunteered?

Not that the community is solely responsible. The process, now blown up out of all sensible proportions, has been helped along by the evangelism of certain religious leaders whose design for the synagogue (or temple) is all-inclusive—a modernized version of the *shul* that dominated life in the European *shtetl*. They see American Jewish life as a spoked wheel, with all of its enterprises radiating from its synagogue hub, in which, centered in all his glory and assumed authority, sits the rabbi. To give substance to this archaic image in an emancipated American Jewish community, the rabbi must turn from an emphasis on worship and religious scholarship to an overmastering emphasis on administrative and organizational activities involving broad community welfare interests.

This process is based on the principle "join-'em-if-you-can't-beat-'em." The modern rabbi, one of the ablest men in the ministry insists, must not only become "the dynamo about whom most forms of positive Jewish values cluster" but also the source "from whom most Jewish activities derive their impetus and direction."

Curiously, what too many rabbis seek as their present-day role is still another paradox of the inclusion of the archaic in the modern. The rabbi-leader of the immigrant congregation may have ignored communal activity outside the synagogue since it was of small consequence in his ghetto community. On the other hand, his counsel was sought and given on any individual's secular problem. It was not unusual for the East Side rabbi (and it still is common practice with the *chassidic rebbe*) to be the final word on a congregant's purchase of a house or investment in securities—notwithstanding that his role of scholar-saint did not qualify the rabbi as a realty appraiser or customer's man.

The modern rabbi, out to fix his role in the changes that have brought non-synagogal institutions into prominence in Jewish life, attempts to firm up his rabbinic authority by hitching community welfare programs to the synagogue and thereby to his domain.

Where non-synagogue activities will not gravitate toward the synagogue and become spokes in its wheel, the "dynamo" rabbi does the gravitating, propelling himself in all directions, in a frantic exhibition of rabbinical ego-imperialism.

There are some rabbis who are aware of the trend and who try to resist it. They strive to avoid the entanglements of the outer institutional life in the community and return to their central purpose of study and scholarship, of encouraging group worship, and of pastoral duties: what a wise Hillel director called "recapturing the human personality of our faith . . . the rabbi as soul speaking to soul" in the fulfillment of his role as counselor and spiritual confidant to the individual Jew and his family. What Jews really need, someone has said, is "a listening rabbi instead of a talking one."

One state-wide rabbinical association, responding to this centripetal impulse, declared that its members must not be expected to deliver invocations and benedictions at public functions. These, the rabbis pointed out, are traditionally the functions of laymen, the rabbi having more serious involvements to command his time.

I sympathize wholeheartedly. I suspect that a good many rabbis, true to their calling, would welcome relief from club luncheons and civic ceremonies. I also suspect that many of them become economic experts and political oracles reluctantly and only because they feel the congregation expects it of them.

The pulpit is the place for inspired teaching. It can provide a prophetic voice for social justice. But when Sabbath homiletics make way for a review of a best-selling novel or an analysis of the Soviet Union's missile program, then I, for one, a dispirited congregant, look around in bewilderment to see whether I am in fact in a pew!

5.

The burden of what I have here mentioned—to nail down my optimism—is my conviction that the American Jewish community, for all its free-wheeling habits, its apathy, its apparent anarchy and controversy and confusion, is still moving on to adulthood. It is not, as some of its critics would have it, hell-bent for oblivion or disintegration. Nor is it doomed to irreligious secularism.

It is a creative community which has evolved its own modern forms of its religion and its own techniques of philanthropy and community welfare. Nostalgic for tradition, it is at once generous, conscious of its defects, liberal in its principles, hospitable to heresy, and always stiff-necked in its persistence.

It is a community with an underlying religious identity; its affiliations with the formal expression of Judaism are growing. Whatever the reasons—whether the need to belong, the comforting security of an emerging American Jewish culture, a sanctuary from the insecurities of a cold-war world, the flexible and enduring strength of Judaism, or any combination of these—the movement toward greater religious activity is meaningful and in keeping with the history of Jewish continuity.

The debates weighing the religious expressions of the Jewish identity vis-à-vis non-synagogal yet still Jewish areas of community life, often called secular, are experiences in forensics and worth the effort for whatever exploration into Jewish values they encourage. But at bottom they are inconclusive, stemming from invalid premises. For what is called secularist is not the antithesis of Judaism but is an integral part of it. There is no contradiction in a simultaneous growth of religious affiliation and so-called secularist activity. Against the background of a free and pluralistic American society with its esteem for individualism and for a multiplicity of differences, both are in harmony.

This is not the same as the "spoked wheel" synagogue community that some religious leaders hold out as the ideal for modern Judaism. Most Jewish community activities are not affiliated with the synagogue. *But their underlying impetus is religious.*

This, of course, is not universally acceptable—and least of all to those who confuse primacy with monopoly in defining religion's role in modern Judaism. Some continue to dismiss most Jewish efforts outside the synagogue as peripheral, remote, and even alien.

Yet, supporting a Jewish hospital or university, joining a Jewish organization, or attending a Hadassah convention are implementations of the religion and synagogue influence of America's Judaism.

It is, in my judgment, shortsighted not to see in these "secular" expressions a cumulative strengthening of religion in Jewish life. It presupposes a narrow competition for Jewish loyalties, struggle rather than cooperation between the synagogue and communal organizations. And the implication left by these exclusivists—to their own detriment—is that the synagogue comes off second best.

I have also met their opposite number. There are men and women in the ranks of my own organization who speak of B'nai B'rith fervently and completely as a "Jewish way of life." I admire their loyalty—and deplore their provincialism. The B'nai B'rith movement, or any equivalent, is neither substitute nor competitor for the synagogue.

Without the synagogue, B'nai B'rith would have no reason to exist. The role of a Jewish organization is that of handmaiden to the fundamental religious striving. It is the instrument for meeting the duty of service and philanthropy that the Jewish faith imposes. It is religion's useful aid for Jewish survival and enrichment.

A friend of mine, a very able rabbi, suggests however—and he is really adamant about it—that in our era of expanding social welfare by government the Jewish community ought to stop fund-raising for Jewish hospitals and clinics, for old-age homes, sanitariums, and similar institutions. He deplores these as wasteful and unnecessary. He gets positively livid (as do so many others) when he considers the millions of community dollars spent each year for Jewish civic defense.

"The pattern is sinful!" he argues. "So much money for such secondary purposes. All of it being diverted from where it belongs—in religious education."

Jewish education needs much more money than it now gets. But what my zealous friend is advocating is to rush to the support of religious education by cancelling out a healthy part of its designed purpose. For in the complex structure of Jewish communal life, dulling the natural desires of well-motivated Jews to build a hospital, to fight anti-Semitism, or even to maintain an agency that hunts down family deserters (yes, we Jews have that kind of social service, too) is to default on the very things our religion seeks to encourage.

It would be tilting with straw men to suggest that my friend reflects a fixed attitude by the rabbinate. The prevailing attitude is far from absolute—"Of course there is a place for Jewish hospitals and Anti-Defamation Leagues in their rightful context," is their lament. "But when they overshadow religious institutions, what happens to religion's primacy?" Others challenge the rationale for Jewish hospitals (and the like) as self-induced forms of second-class citizenship in a democratic and egalitarian society. Why must Jews, they ask, finance hospitals and non-sectarian universities— a function of the American community as a whole?

These are essentially defensive rationalizations and therefore negative; they spring from an unwarranted urge by some elements of our religious leadership to *impose* a primacy for religious institutions over other forms of expressing our Judaism. Their effect, however, is always to stir up a contest, a competition between the synagogue and Jewish extra-synagogal interests. The observable truth, however, is that the Jew who has completely forsaken his Judaism finds no compulsion or purpose in supporting a Jewish hospital or Jewish civic defense agency. The out-and-out assimilationist has abandoned these, as well as the synagogue. The Jew to whom these institutions are expressive of his Jewishness, even though he is neglectful of the synagogue, is certainly not endangering the synagogue.*

Curiously, some of the extreme voices that condemn Jewish social service on "egalitarian principles" also speak in terms of a Jewish enclave in America unhampered by secularism—and these voices are somewhat bitter about the egalitarianism that allows Jews freedom *from* organized religion.

With its parent the synagogue, Jewish education is part of reli-

---

* This is not to be taken as advocating an immutable continuity of secular Jewish institutions as against their absorption by the general community. It is an interesting historical fact that B'nai B'rith, the first American organization to institute voluntary disaster relief, bowed out with the development of the American National Red Cross. The same is true for most of the orphanages and old-age homes which B'nai B'rith founded in its early years. But these changes are a separate issue, one predicated on the shifting patterns in American life, and completely unrelated to the false issue of religion in competition with Jewish secularism.

gion's pulse-beat in Jewish life. Its importance, however, is not likely to be respected in the practical terms religious leaders and educators are pleading for as long as their formula involves compromising or repressing other Jewish institutions.

The sound procedure is not to advance education by denigrating other institutions and values. Reduced support for hospitals and civic defense will not, of itself, mean more for religion and religious education. It may have the very opposite effect of reducing the enthusiasm and sense of identification on which all forms of Jewish activity thrive. To meet new obligations, American Jews need only to have their ardor for their identity sustained, not stultified or strapped into a cramping pattern.

That task represents a challenge for our religious leaders.

# (2)

## *When You've Got the Votes . . . Don't Use Them*

There is an ancient legend about the Septuagint, the translation of
the Pentateuch into Greek. Ptolemy II of Egypt enlisted seventy-
two Hebrew scholars from Palestine for the task, isolated them in
seventy-two rooms where they labored seventy-two days, and when
they emerged, lo—these seventy-two translations were identical
in every word.

This news spread quickly through the gathering places of Alex-
andria.

"Remarkable!" said the pagans in the market place.

"Miraculous!" said the gossipers at the public baths.

"Amazing Jewish unity!" said the king.

Later Jewish experience has provided a cynical addition to the legend. "The scholars were kept separate, weren't they? If seventy-two Jews in the *same* room agreed—that would be a miracle!"

There is a sure way to set off explosive opinions in Jewish life. Just ask: "When will American Jewry be united? Why can't the community end its anarchy and chaos and put its house in order?"

Here is an issue that never falters, never retreats into obscurity, never flags. It is a constant, evergreen, durable as is tradition itself.

It *is* a tradition. American Jews have been sounding a tocsin for unity ever since enough of them were settled on these shores and found an abundance of things to disagree on.

Everybody is for unity. What goal is more righteous or obvious in Jewish life? We are enraptured of unity's virtues (if frustrated by its elusiveness). So much so that we stand ready to argue and persuade, to bludgeon and, finally, forcibly vote to have the other fellow accept our concept and discipline of unity.

It has since become an inevitable paradox that Jewish polemics are noisiest and at their most passionate and even violent when the subject is "unity" in Jewish affairs.

Yet the theme of unity persists. There is no sturdier topic for convention resolutions or impassioned letters to editors of the English-Jewish press. In the more than thirty-year span of my own adult activities I have heard—and occasionally shared—this dismay at what the penetrating Rabbi Milton Steinberg called "the howling topsy-turvydom" of Jewish life.

True, we Jews live in "overorganized confusion." We have fathered some three hundred national organizations, many of them "national" fully as far west as Hoboken, New Jersey. We have produced an even greater number of regional and local community councils and welfare funds, and an uncounted progeny of Jewish social clubs, communal services, burial societies, *landsmanshaften,* synagogue centers, welfare agencies, professional groups, and bowling leagues—enough to bewilder the most intrepid statistician. A complete census of independent Jewish causes, social and communal, religious and secular, local and national, would be a monumental exercise in statistical analysis. All to prove that there is a Jewish organization to satisfy every point of view and a plethora of views testifying to the historic stiff-necked independence of the Jewish character.

Meanwhile, the care and feeding of this brawling progeny is not without its burdens. The voice of the total community can become lost in the babel of a thousand tongues.

As a young man on the periphery of Jewish affairs I was captivated by the image of an orderly unified community. A disciplined and democratized tidiness was, it seemed to me, the key to releasing Jewish life from confusions, competitions, and over-lappings.

I was encouraged in this view by the emerging era when American Jewry, its source of replenishment from abroad cut off by restrictive immigration, was plainly destined to lose its variegated European colorations. What was to become of us? Were we to vanish in assimilation? Or could we be sustained by a new creative culture of our own?

Here was the fork in the road. But how were we to advance down the path of a native and homogenous Jewish culture without a coalescence of our scattered forces? The future cried out for unity—order out of chaos!

This, the uncompromising, confident, wisdom of my youth was in a measure affected by geography. My environment was a Midwesterner's and Jewish life in Omaha, as detached and self-insulating as in Manhattan's overpopulated ghetto, or among the Jewish parochialists of the West Coast, or for the isolated "first Jewish families" of the South, seemed capable of an orderly process of unification.

It was natural, perhaps, to appraise the diverse and ethnic-segregated character of American Jewry as a "wild anarchy" instead of as a living expression of man's infinite variety, and then to compound the error by confusing unity with unification. There were examples around to support this drastic conviction. Had not American Jewry spoken with a single voice at the Versailles peace table through its American Jewish Congress?* Was there not an all-embracing, if loosely defined Zionism in its first flush of post-World War I popularity? Was there not the federation movement?† In these developments I found the logic for a symmetrical community with rules to provide for every Jewish impulse.

Of course, these were exceptions to what was—or so I thought of it—rambunctious anarchy. Vigilant as the next critic of the diverse and scattered, I rallied to the cry of "Unity!" And when ballots were called for, I cast mine in its favor.

I don't anymore. Experience has taught me a stubborn, inescapable truth about unity. It cannot be *voted* into existence.

I have not lost my youthful trust in the virtues of coordination, of orderliness, and even of measured degrees of unity in Jewish affairs.

I have changed my approach to them and my judgment as to their values, measured by their costs.

Several times in my lifetime American Jewry was afflicted with wide-ranging strife, all in the name of unity. More than once each contesting side crowed that it had won the battle. The fact is that these struggles inevitably are without a victor. There is only a loser—the community itself.

The history of the pressures for unity in American Jewry shows a consistent course. There is an emergency to trigger the demand for unity. The emergency subsides; the effort collapses. This is history. We fail to recognize that American Jewry, steeped in its environmental freedoms, can only cooperate voluntarily and through means appropriate to its American milieu.

---

* The American Jewish Congress, convened in 1917 as a temporary body to lobby for minority rights convenants in World War I peace treaties, represented a successful revolt of the East European wing of American Jewry from the dominant leadership of the longer-settled, more affluent and influential, but smaller German wing. The Congress comprised community-elected delegates as well as representatives of national Jewish groups. By prearrangement it dissolved in 1920. The present American Jewish Congress was founded in 1922.

† Some views on Jewish fund raising are related in Chapter 5.

The fact that an emancipated Jewish community responds to discipline only in moments of emergency perhaps marks its unpreparedness for emergency. But if this is true it is a fault typically American.

It is characteristic of democracy, with its varieties and its basic voluntarism, to appear immobilized. We have been consistently unprepared for wars and economic depressions. But just as consistently we have been equal to them, although in the process we have learned that the cost of the free society comes high. What is more natural than for the American Jewish community to behave as America itself does? To pay as heavy a price for its fluidity and for the noisy cacophony of its many voices? And to experience the same ultimate triumphs?

There still lingers, here and there, the once more popular notion that we can, by our own free will, fit the shape of our community's pre-bred democracy into the mold of the Old World *kehilla*. This sentiment is blind to the fact that the East European *kehilla* was an outgrowth of gentile oppressions and of the civic—and legal—inferiority of Jews. The *kehilla* was an official Jewish acceptance of the reality of a ghetto enclave, physically and psychologically. In most cases it was endowed by the state with legal powers. And without these coercive powers, majority rule in a free society is inoperative.

The totality of all freedom is measured by its self-imposed limitations. The greater the freedom the greater the dissidence. We cannot have the one without the other. A Jewish community that attempts to strengthen its identity by the forcible imposition of majority rule can't beat down this principle. Not without a policeman's club—that it hasn't got. And never will have so long as the American concept of freedom endures.

2.

In the beginning there were the Sephardim. The first Ashkenazic Jews trickled into colonial America soon afterward. Here were two disparate groups separated in the Old World by differences in custom, language, and culture. In the colonies they were as one, for the best of reasons: they were too few in forces to make their differences count.

By 1825 there were six thousand Jews in America. The Ashkenazim, by then a substantial majority, felt strong enough to break away from Sephardic domination; they organized their own synagogue, setting up *their own* kind of Jewish community. It developed out of a small rebellion over a trifling difference. But it became a milestone. From that day on, in one form or another, American Jewry has been organizationally variegated. Its growth-roots reach down into a nourishing wellspring of individualism and dissent. And, significantly, it has flourished.

The Ashkenazic community itself was soon splintered by ethnic self-segregations of immigrants from Prussia, Bohemia, and Bavaria who, beginning in the 1830's, arrived in large numbers. Each group established a synagogue-community rooted in its own European origins.

When, after several generations, many units of Jewish life found a common, unifying, milieu in Reform Judaism they set about to embrace their scattered elements in a nation-wide movement, the Union of American Hebrew Congregations. The Union, founded in 1873, gave rise to Hebrew Union College and both institutions have endured as a central force in Reform Judaism. This was, however, not their founders' purpose. For they began as an experiment in unity between traditionalist (both Sephardic and Ashkenazic) and liberal Jews. No less a spokesman for traditional Judaism than the indomitable Isaac Leeser, first translator of the Hebrew Bible into English, subordinated his distaste for Reform to his faith in an organized unity. He himself died before the Union and the College were established, but traditionalists who shared his convictions on unity joined with Reform leaders to initiate both institutions. This harmony lasted less than twelve years. When the Reform rabbinate of the Union enunciated its Pittsburgh Platform, setting forth principles of liberal Judaism that the followers of Leeser found totally incompatible with traditionalist belief, the traditionalists stepped out, realigned, and established the Jewish Theological Seminary, the first of the national institutions of Conservative Judaism.*

Had the Union sustained its original character, its purpose—to speak for a united American Jewry—would have foundered on another development: the onrush of East European Jewish immigrants who brought their own backgrounds and customs with them. The Orthodoxy of the newcomers clashed with the Reform of native American Jews. Even those immigrants whose radicalism made them passive or hostile toward their Orthodox background kept their distance from a Reform Judaism they knew little about and that gave no signs of wanting to know about them. The radicalism, the *Yiddishism,* and the Zionism imported by these East Europeans—issues on which the new immigrants themselves differed, but that were of vital meaning to them—collided with the views of the older Americans of Sephardic and German stock.

Until at least a generation after World War I American Jewry was polyglot and correspondingly caste-ridden. The frowns against intermarriage between a German-ancestored Jew and one of East European origin were often as grim and forboding as those against intermarriage between Jew and Christian. There were crude Yiddish jokes on supposedly mutual antipathies of Lithuanian and Galician Jews. Differences were many, often transitory but occasionally deep and meaningful, extending beyond those of wealth and social status. There were differences in sociological outlook, religious philosophy, convictions about Jewish nationalism.

All this was a major roadblock to unity. But while it encouraged separatism it also repulsed conformity. In giving the Jewish community a stratified and disparate character, it also evoked its creative vitality. The first three decades of the twentieth century are historic testimony to the enormous contributions both to American

* The founders of the Seminary expected that their cause would be endorsed by the Orthodox immigrants of Eastern Europe since both elements were loyal to traditional Judaism. This hope was soon wrecked by the pronounced ethnic and cultural differences between the groups. Orthodoxy went its own way, setting up its own distinctive institutions.

civilization and to Jewish survival made by the "topsy-turvydom" of Jewish life.

Much has happened since those vital—if bewildering—years.

More and more the veneers of Old World colorations are stripped away as native-born American Jews and their children grow up as an essentially middle-class American society. Each successive Jewish generation reduces the sharp edges of the immigrant difference and encourages the prospect of greater coherence in the community. The trend is toward stability in status and culture; even toward sameness. This is a force for maturity—and unity—in communal life but it is not without its price, as anyone who has marveled at the artistry of Maurice Schwartz and Molly Picon, or at the language and world of Sholem Aleichem, must acknowledge with sorrow. Thus, the fate of Yiddish—an irreparable loss—appears sealed although zealots among the Yiddishists will deny this.

### 3.

So which do we want—a unified community or a lively one?

A natural human answer is that we want the best of both. This we cannot have by any Messianic approach to a compulsive unity —even if it could be realized in a voluntary society.

The hazard in discussing Jewish unity is that we deal with a vague term: "unity" is whatever its definer wants it to mean. Chameleon-like, it takes on one coloration in Jewish fund raising ("philanthropy should be federated to reduce wasteful competition"), another in Jewish defense ("community relations agencies should divide their duties and agree on a common course of action"), still another in religious Judaism ("Jews should unite through the synagogue—that is, through *my* denomination"). National organizations and local community councils each can spell out a meaning for unity and the definitions would turn out to be poles apart.

We tend to misplace a basic fact of unity. It is *not* a goal. It is a *state of affairs*. If Jewish community life must define its goal let us just say that we want the community to be venturesome and alive. We make mischief of unity when we ignore its illusory character and treat it as an end in itself. It is no paradox, therefore, when our galloping efforts toward unity serve the contradictory purpose of running it into the ground.

Senator Clifford Case once wrote of freedom as "something that can never be finally won, it can only be lost." This can be paraphrased for Jewish unity in a free society; unity has no absolutes, only degrees. It is a contradiction of unity when it is exploited to impose a single, even a compromise, conclusion. For in a free society, unity has its natural limitation: *it can create a setting where common conclusions might be accepted; it can do no more.* Only when the process of voluntary adherence is recognized, when we abandon efforts to apply enforcement powers, can we attain its maximum substance. The really valid product of unity is—*cooperation.* This may exclude coalescing or compromising on divergent, deeply-felt opinions. It can mean a framework in which different viewpoints may find some common if limited areas of agreement.

A voluntary Jewish community must make room for difference, for dissidence, and for challenge to the status quo and to the entrenched institutions. These are freedom's catalysts for progress. "There is only one thing in life about which there can be no controversy; the right of, and need for, controversy." * This rule applies to Jewish unity. We need not surrender to chaos or collapse into a stultifying uniformity; to tolerate, even to encourage, dissent is a worthier goal. If this is asking too much, the absolute minimum is not to *discourage* dissent.

It is a mere pretense of unity—a meaningless ritual play—when unity is reduced to concurrence among the like-minded and its imposition upon others; or when it rejects a process in which divergent views interact in a forum untrammeled by "majority rule" dominance. For Jewish life, the first prerequisite of unity is to involve the community—to express the participation in Jewish af-

---

* Dr. Buell Gallagher, president of the City College of New York, said it in 1953 in a memorable Freedom Forum address sponsored by the Anti-Defamation League of B'nai B'rith.

fairs of many Jews and as many diverse philosophies. Unity that speaks for a fraction, however large, of Jewish life and that leaves the rest voiceless, is a contradiction in terms.

The American Council for Judaism is, to my mind, an organization whose frenzied actions—as distinct from its credo—abuse the philosophy it advertises on its letterhead. Is it a disruptive force in the community? The overwhelmingly pro-Israel sentiment of American Jewry would contend that it is. Yet the existence of the Council is an element to be considered in the agitation for Jewish unity. So long as its proponents (however splintered a minority) maintain a point of view (however schizophrenic*), the absence of the Council (or a similar group) would be to throw a pall of silence, indifference or passivity over the community.

The value of the Council to Jewish community life is that it ventilates a dissenting point of view, a stimulus that invites the counterstimulant of opposition to its view. In the colliding process the community grows with an increase of vitality for the majority view.

No one deliberately seeks out opposition. But where its exists, its ventilation tends to strengthen, or at least refine, the thinking of the majority. This is one of the gifts of freedom.

4.

The expurgators of disorder in Jewish life are forever proving Santayana's law: unwilling to learn from history they doom themselves to repeating it. The community's history is littered with many battles, few triumphs, fought in the name of unity.

The single area where persistent pressure for organic unity has made an appreciable advance is philanthropy, this through the

---

* It screams of an "American" Judaism at the same time that it protests overriding allegiance to a *universalism* in Judaism. It glorifies the integration of Jews into the American society while italicizing the *individual* Jew and his *individual* quality.

growth of federated fund raising.* Meanwhile, the great promise of
the past twenty-five years, the development of community councils,
is still unrealized. There are many local councils, each with its own
pattern. Some are approximations of community unity; others are
contradictions of it.

Why has it more or less worked in fund raising? Jewish philanthropy has a non-controversial quality; there are no intense ideological differences. Moreover, the united fund offers, at least in
theory, economies in fund raising.

The same arguments have been advanced to encourage organic
unity in Jewish civic defense programs. Nowhere have efforts to
bring "order out of chaos" been made so persistently as in the field
of community relations. And just as consistently these have failed.

The success in the one area and the failure in the other—both
illuminate the nature of the problem of unity in Jewish life.

It is true that civic defense has mass appeal. What Jew who is
not an out-and-out apostate is unconcerned with anti-Semitism?
The immediacy of the problem during the Hitler era raised civic
defense from small expenditures and modest projects to million-
dollar educational programs and staffs probing vast hitherto-
unexplored areas of human relations. The diminished strength and
decline in overt manifestation of anti-Semitism in the postwar
period, reinforced by the advent of Israel's statehood, have reduced Jews' concern about their physical safety. But with civic
defense embracing the broader scope of civil liberties and human
rights, its support is as popularly based as ever.

Yet while civic defense has the same universal appeal as philanthropy, unlike philanthropy, it has resisted efforts to make it

---

* Even federated fund raising resisted being overunified through a plan for
compulsory national budgeting. This proposed that local federations and
welfare funds refrain from independent judgment and instead allocate their
funds in strict accordance with a nation-wide formula that would be promul-
gated by the Council of Jewish Federations and Welfare Funds. The issue
was soundly defeated at the 1941 CJFWF national assembly in Atlanta. Had
the mandatory plan carried, it is doubtful that CJFWF could have survived
the ensuing revolts of local federations and the agencies they raise funds
for, each jealous, and properly so, of its prerogatives.

a single community institution. In theory there may be no deep philosophical conflicts in the community about fighting anti-Semitism. In practice—that is, in methodology and techniques—there are viewpoints that acquire the force of ideology.

The century-long history of organized Jewish defense has an instructive pattern. The beginning of each civic defense group was a case of the community—or its active segments—uniting to fight anti-Semitism. When the group had common roots—the conservative, affluent, "old stock" German Jewry that created the American Jewish Committee or the Yiddish-speaking, union-centered Eastern Europeans of the Jewish Labor Committee—it survived. When dissimilar elements were pressed to join in a conformist mold, the attempt failed.

This was the fate of the Board of Delegates of American Israelites, organized in 1859, the first Jewish defense agency in the United States. As with most of its successors, it arrived in the wake of an "emergency"—the Mortara kidnapping—primarily to engage in anti-discrimination work and "promote the unity of American Jewry." It fell apart within a generation—unable to achieve a common working basis among its founders and constituents who were separated by ethnic barriers and divided over the Reform-traditionalist conflict in religious ideologies.

The first (1917) American Jewish Congress was an ambitious attempt at unity that lasted long enough to achieve its immediate purpose of incorporating Jewish "group rights" provisions in the peace treaties following World War I. The unity endured as long as did the urgency of its purpose—and no longer. The effort of Rabbi Stephen Wise to continue the movement by a "majority rule" vote was defeated. A rump meeting of the group presided over by Wise did establish the present American Jewish Congress as a middle-class, Zionist-minded group, partially representative of the late migrations from Eastern Europe, but it was and is only a splinter faction of the original Congress.

The American Jewish Conference of 1943 was a coordinative effort that lasted four years. Hitler's downfall and the convulsive aftermath of a world war had dropped a multitude of problems in the lap of American Jewry. The Jewish communities of Europe were decimated, their remnants scattered in DP camps. A staggering task of rescue and resettlement, a task complicated by the British White Paper restricting Jewish immigration to Palestine, needed the articulate voice and the strength of a united Jewry. With this in mind, Henry Monsky, then president of B'nai B'rith, issued his "Pittsburgh call," to which thirty-two national Jewish bodies responded. Once again, provision was made for electing delegates from the major Jewish communities.

The Conference was called to deal with the foreseeable emergency problems of the postwar era. Its scope was limited, its life was to be temporary, its permanency was never agreed to. (The American Jewish Committee and the Jewish Labor Committee consented to participate only if the Conference remained an *ad hoc* organization.) In so large a body, representing almost the totality of organized Jewish life, there were zealots for uniting Jews by "majority rule" who were blind to the pitfalls. The temporary nature of the Conference was often obscured by excessive formality and procedures that encouraged "bloc" voting. This carry-over from East European patterns directed excessive attention to ideological differences among the Conference's constituent groups and helped accelerate its demise. A sounder practice would have stressed what they held in common.

The actual breakup came when the Conference proposed to permanentize itself under the name of the American Jewish Assembly. Several major constituents, B'nai B'rith among them, refused to accept the Assembly's existence and the Conference soon disappeared—one more case history to mark the failure of attempts at enforced unity.*

* A B'nai B'rith Committee of Sixty-Four, embracing every geographic segment of the organization, met to consider the proposed American Jewish Assembly. Its deliberations were exhaustive and without rancor. I argued strongly for affiliation—once again, as in the past, finding myself in the minority on the "unity issue." By that time I recognized the frailty and ineffectiveness of roof organizations that tried to live by majority rule. But the collective strength of the Conference in an era of major political upheavals destined to affect Jewish life throughout the world seemed to me of overriding importance.

Some historians have called the American Jewish Conference a failure. This is not an accurate appraisal since it ignores the impermanent and

## 5.

I can understand the tourist in Atlantic City tumbling into bed at six o'clock in the morning after a night of gaiety. But where is the good sense of the delegate who stays awake through the long hours of the night, cramped in a hotel room, trading arguments on the dialectics of Jewish unity?

Still, I was one of the stay-awakes.

This was 1951. The subject of the debate was an apparently mild document on Jewish community relations, called the Mac-Iver Report after its author, Dr. Robert I. MacIver of Columbia University. A scholar and sociologist, he had conducted a twenty-five-thousand-dollar survey financed by the Large Cities Budgeting Conference, a coalition of the larger Jewish community welfare funds.

In his survey, Professor MacIver made no startling discoveries. What he reported was a condition long visible—that the six national agencies and twenty-nine community councils then affiliated with the National Community Relations Advisory Council, a consultative forum for civic defense groups, were involved in jurisdictional disputes, competing for funds and often duplicating one another's functions.*

Dr. MacIver's obvious, well-intentioned, if somewhat costly, homily became the springboard for a well-advertised campaign to

---

emergency character of the Conference. In much of its planning, in its testimony before the Anglo-American inquiry on partition of Palestine, in its representation to the Government, appeals to the American public, and other programs, the Conference expressed, clearly and strongly, a viewpoint shared by almost the entire Jewish community.

* National agencies enrolled in NCRAC at the time of the MacIver Report were the Anti-Defamation League of B'nai B'rith, American Jewish Committee, American Jewish Congress, Jewish Labor Committee, Jewish War Veterans, and Union of American Hebrew Congregations. NCRAC was founded in 1944 as successor to the ill-fated General Jewish Council, a similar effort to coordinate Jewish defense work that constituted the programs of the first four of the above agencies. Neither by temperament nor tradition were its constituents conditioned for the give-and-take of the compromise. The General Jewish Council came a cropper when the agencies split over the "hush-hush" policy of combating anti-Semitism.

"end waste and duplication" in civic defense. Since the total budget for this activity exceeded five million dollars a year, the shout of "unity!" rose in many throats. Rabbis who would be horrified at a suggestion that denominationalized Judaism—with its minimally triplicating administrative machinery, its competing congregational classrooms, and its three cantorial schools doing the work of one—might gain by some form of consolidation, used the pulpit to urge this course for civic defense agencies. Some leaders of federations and welfare funds, pressed to increase their overseas contributions, seized upon the report as an excuse to reduce allocations to civic defense groups. Community councils liked it for the increased status it proposed for them. The MacIver Report became a handy club to enforce compulsory unity.

But far from uniting Jewish defense it split the community wide open.

In much of its content, the MacIver Report seemed to me to be a too, too simple document. The researcher's impartiality was countered by his lack of close familiarity with American Jewish history and life. In sum, the report produced two things. A disruptive issue, with a good part of the Jewish community taking sides—although not more than one out of a hundred who pontificated had ever read the MacIver Report. And a series of specific proposals, not in themselves revolutionary or grievously inequitable, but also, as has since been shown, not particularly relevant.

MacIver acknowledged, but with curious detachment, that the abundance of defense agencies was something more than caprice, that each sprang from its own background and that they reflected the "irreconcilable social and economic differences" of their supporters. But he also argued that these differences were tangential to the common cause against anti-Semitism.

Yet MacIver hesitated to extend his argument to a logical conclusion—the substitution of a single, all-embracing defense agency for the multiplicity that existed. Acting perhaps out of realistic prudence (none of the agencies was disposed to suicide), MacIver arrived at a meaningless compromise. He proposed a not-so-clear-cut separation of responsibilities—the Anti-Defamation League to have primacy in investigative and counteraction programming, the American Jewish Congress to work in the legislative and litigative fields, the Union of American Hebrew Congregations to handle inter-religious programming, and so forth.

To enforce these arbitrary separations and to guard against encroachments, he proposed that a roof organization, the National Community Relations Advisory Council, have standing committees that would control the process of coordination and settle jurisdictional disputes. Thus, what began as an advisory council was now to take on the character of a functioning agency. Instead of decreasing the number of defense groups, MacIver's recommendations ended up by adding another.

Without cynicism, it can be said that the MacIver dispute evolved as a struggle between *haves* and *have nots,* a conflict not unique in human, or organizational, affairs. The less affluent members of NCRAC seemed delighted with the proposals. Each was to get a bigger piece of the activity pie and the funds that went with it. The two largest defense agencies, the Anti-Defamation League and the American Jewish Committee, each of which had a comprehensive far-reaching community relations program in many areas, challenged a course of action that would merely truncate their programs while enlarging the activities of the other organizations. How would this improve matters? they wanted to know.

The struggle went on for several years. All of the persuasive language appeals—to "end duplication," "stop waste"—were there to help those who campaigned to put several of the MacIver recommendations (though drastically modified) into effect. The opposing argument—that in the American tradition of voluntary association no one, outside of its own constituency, can compel an organization to change its strategy or tactics and certainly not its ideology—could not match the appeal of the well-advertised catch phrases.

But as the years passed, the substantive issue became lost in the jungle of strongly held convictions and stronger words. At the second of two NCRAC annual assemblies in Atlantic City to wrestle with the problem, the opposing sides no longer had anything in common to outweigh the firm belief each had in its own rectitude.

The issue was then brought to a vote—the most ill-advised move of all. A combination of national agencies and community councils easily outvoted the Anti-Defamation League and the American Jewish Committee with, as the only result, a withdrawal of the two from their affiliation with NCRAC.

Once again, an effort to impose unity had achieved a more determined separation.

The morning after the disastrous meeting, I breakfasted with a community council leader who had initiated the vote. He was crestfallen by his Pyrrhic victory. I reminded him of a useful political rule. "In a voluntary movement, when you've got the votes, don't use them. That's the time to keep negotiating."

6.

I met Dr. Nahum Goldmann for the first time a few months after my election in 1953 as president of B'nai B'rith. There has since developed a warm personal relationship between us. Cultured, mild-spoken, yet often iconclastic, Dr. Goldmann is a fascinating personality, a fusion of the urbane diplomat and the precinct-conscious politician. The scope of Jewish activities spreads across large areas of the world, and many are deep in one or more of their aspects; Goldmann is immersed in all of them. He wears many hats: he is chairman of the Jewish Agency for Israel; president of the World Jewish Congress; chairman of the Conference of Jewish Material Claims Against Germany; a member of countless committees.

I do not always agree with Goldmann. His convictions are those of political Zionism, a philosophy I do not share. Our ideological outlooks on Jewish life are often at opposite ends. But he is a sophisticate; his judgment is mature, his mind facile and objective. Above all, he is a realist.

One day, eight years ago, we met for a private talk.

"Klutznick," he began, "now is the time to revive something similar to the American Jewish Conference."

I must have frowned.

"Now wait," he continued. "Think about it for a moment. Forget the past and measure the present. Israel exists today as a state and all of us, except perhaps the American Council for Judaism, support it. There are no *real* differences separating us on that question, are there? This is a critical period in Jewish history. American Jews must join forces and do their thinking together on it."

This was the unity argument—again. Goldmann had sprung it on me abruptly, although by pure coincidence I was not entirely unprepared.

A few weeks earlier, I had parried, as premature, a plea from the NCRAC urging the return of B'nai B'rith and its Anti-Defamation League. I was still probing my way as a new president, and the invitation led me into a search for a middle path between the failures of coercive unity, the weakness of *ad hoc* arrangements, and the dismal prospects when there is no cooperation at all. I put my ideas into a public address in which I said:

As with Moses and the children of Israel, we have been wandering in the desert for more than the Biblical forty years. What we need first and foremost is a realistic approach that will recognize the validity of the mistakes of yesterday. We need a *first* step toward the goal of maximum cooperation, one that will take full cognizance of the voluntary character of our community. We need, then, a place where we can learn to know each other better. Not only do most of us need Jewish education, we need education about Jews—their ideologies, their institutions, their organizations. Whether we agree with each other or not is not half as important as that we learn through knowledge of each other to respect one another. It would be hard for you to believe that only a few weeks ago I was with the national presidents of two very prominent Jewish organizations. Each man had served for four or more years as president. They had never met. It was my prvilege to introduce one to the other.

So what I would suggest, first of all, is that the men who lead our communal organizations get to know each other, get to talk informally and without the encumbrances of staff and protocol. I think it would be a good thing for the community if the presidents of every national Jewish organization—and only the presidents, no substitutes—were to meet with each other at least four times a year. Such a meeting-group would need no staff and no budget. . . . There would be no voting except by objection, and no action unless agreement was unanimous.

There are those, of course, who would say, "What about local representation?" Now, we have tried that in both the American Jewish Conference and the NCRAC. This is reaching for the ultimate and becomes a point of bitter contention. I am not proposing the ultimate. I am not proposing that we try to create an assembly, or a congress, for long-term functioning.

People who insist upon a congress, a *kehilla*, or a conference will call this kind of meeting "milk and water." To them I can only say it is less than you want and more than you have. It fills a void.

This was my counter-proposal to Goldmann—a loose, informal gathering of organization presidents; no budget; no administrative machinery; no staff; not even, at the start, an address; and no "majority rule."

Goldmann preferred something closer to the American Jewish Conference, although more limited in purpose. But when we reviewed the national organizations that might be disposed to join —recognizing the need to keep a new movement small enough to be effective, yet large enough to be representative of the organized community—he conceded the difficulties of accommodating their traditional differences in a formalized assembly. He agreed that, as a fresh approach, what I had outlined was worth a try.

In March 1954 a loose-knit group of sixteen organization presidents held its first meeting.* There were no identifying

---

* The sixteen organizations were: American Jewish Congress, American Trade Union Council for Labor Israel, American Israel Committee for Public Affairs, American Zionist Council, B'nai B'rith, Hadassah, Jewish Agency for Israel (American Section), Jewish Labor Committee, Jewish War Veterans, Labor Zionist Organization of America, Mizrachi Organization of America, National Community Relations Advisory Council, Union of American Hebrew Congregations, Union of Orthodox Jewish Congregations, United Synagogue of America, and Zionist Organization of America. The National Council of Jewish Women joined soon afterwards, followed (1960) by the National Council of Young Israel. The Council of Jewish Federations and Welfare funds is an observer.

The American Jewish Committee resisted affiliation. The flexible character of the group did not appear to me in conflict with the Committee's freedom of action or its traditional aloofness toward what one of its leaders called symbols except a labored title, THE CONFERENCE OF PRESIDENTS OF MAJOR JEWISH ORGANIZATIONS—since popularized as "The Presidents' Conference."

It has survived for almost seven years, a period in which the emotional tremors of American Jewry were registered in all directions. The cold war descended on the Middle East and the American Jewish community looked on with a mixture of pride, concern and even anguish as Israel struggled to find its bearings amid the patchwork diplomacy of the Western powers. It was an era of one crisis treading sharp on the heels of another—and this reality proved to be the binding force to keep the Presidents' Conference together.

Seventeen (after the National Council of Jewish Women had joined) national presidents around a single table can be a massing of sensitive egos. However, by resisting all forms of coercion, the Presidents' Conference was spared the awkwardness of organizational rivalries or personal jealousies. Anyone who disagreed could say so. No one was criticized for violating nonexistent by-laws. Anyone who wanted to walk out could leave without challenge.

There have been disagreements within the Presidents' Conference. But no one has ever walked out.

The fact that there has been a single area of reference—the relationships between American Jewry and Israel; in particular, issues that are quasi-political rather than cultural or philanthropic —has been a unifying force. The group has steered clear of extraneous issues.

There have been no fixed meeting dates. The group assembled only when contingencies dictated. In periods of critical stress—

---

"entangling alliances." I tried to so persuade Irving Engel, the Committee's president, and even offered to nominate him as chairman of the new group. But the administrative board of the American Jewish Committee rejected affiliation.

In retrospect, I probably erred, as did others, in our pleadings with the American Jewish Committee. The effect could have been to exaggerate the importance of any single organization. It was important that we involve the largest possible concentration of major organizations. But not everyone needed to belong. It was more important that those who did join were sincerely eager to get along with one another.

as in the Sinai outbreak of October 1956—there were meetings several times a week.

There has been a cross-fertilization in exchange of information and ideas. The presidents not only learned about one another, but from each other. This, it seems to me, was a necessary, if sometimes faltering step toward the enduring task of keeping the Jewish community intellectually alert to its own problems.

Talking together has led to acting together: in public statements, in community meetings, in consultations with the State Department and other Government agencies, in developing helpful personal relationships in the delicate area of international affairs. All of these, in their cumulative effect, have given articulation and a salutary measure of guidance to a Jewish community that might otherwise have been confused by its own good intentions toward Israel, or that might have dissipated its power by weak internal communications or the wasteful strife of competition.

How long the Presidents' Conference, with its unshapen format, will continue to exist is a question. It can, of course, destroy itself on the shoals of personal antagonisms among its president-members. Or it can succumb to philosophical disagreements. It could, hopefully, find itself without direct purpose should a tranquil Middle East be realized.

On the other hand, it may carry on for many years. It could widen its area of interest, or recast itself into a formalized body (there have been some steps in this direction) bringing, to a modest degree, the advantages of an organizational structure. Hopefully, it may continue without stumbling into the pitfalls of coerced conformity or superauthoritarianism in Jewish life.

But this is conjecture. Whatever its ultimate fate, the Presidents' Conference, in its modest experience, has demonstrated that voluntary cooperation is as feasible a goal as fully organic unity is an infinitely extended controversial issue.

### 7.

"The spirit of Judaism," said Moses Mendelssohn, "is conformity in deed and freedom in dogma." So long as the tradition of Talmudic debate remains a Jewish quality—two Jews arguing three sides of the question—we can expect, with a sense of relief, that Jewish life will resist any precut patterns.

The great strength of Jewish life historically has been its vigorous independence. The story is told that when Ben-Gurion visited Harry Truman, the former President asked him how a new country such as Israel, with all of the dangers surrounding it, could afford the luxury of a Cabinet crisis. Ben-Gurion replied: "In the United States, Mr. President, you have more than 150 million people and one President; in Israel we have one million two hundred thousand people and one million two hundred thousand presidents."

American Jews all have a share in this historic stance of "stiff-necked" independence. Yet, however free-wheeling the Jewish impulses, there is a common desire on the part of most Jews to strengthen the bonds of their community. So patently true is this that, in the last generation or so, new instruments of community cooperation have been devised and sustained. In fund raising, in the Jewish center movement, in some phases of religious education and, more latterly, in the case of the Presidents' Conference, a pattern has emerged by which cooperation has been mutual, freely entered, freely accepted. These illustrate the kind of structure for cooperation that is indigenous to American life.

There is a delightful story of a Jewish couple who took their three sons to *shul* for Simhas Torah. The youngsters were enthralled with the festive spirit that fills the synagogue for the "Rejoicing in the Law." Returning home, they fashioned their own Torahs—some books wrapped in towels—imagined the living room as a sanctuary and played *shul* by marching around the room, singing holiday songs.

When their parents looked in a half hour later, only two were in the living room. The youngest was marching and singing around the dining room table.

"What happened?"

"They won't sing the song I want to sing. We voted and I lost."

"Why are you in the dining room?"

"I started my own *shul!*"

Two shuls in the place of one remains a problem in Jewish life. But what if Mama had enforced the "majority rule" and the only alternative for her youngest, denied his own *shul,* was to passively ignore his brothers' game?

I prefer two *shuls.* In the right spirit and setting, they might find some grounds for cooperation and, in time, even unite their two *shuls* into one.

If I seem to oversimplify it is only to bring the realities into sharp focus and to suggest that our experiences offer a profound lesson to Jewish leadership. All-or-nothing planners in Jewish life had best be disregarded; their extremism is unworkable. On the one hand, the outworn notion that the destiny of American Jewry must be placed in the hands of those anointed with wealth, business or political position, and social prestige, is a modern replica of the *stadtlonism* of yesteryear. Some Jews adhere to this viewpoint actively and some adopt it out of sheer apathy. But it is as decadent as is paternalism of every type. The other extreme is the well-motivated but haplessly impossible concept of a modern *kehilla* that can, despite its origins under totally different circumstances, somehow be made to conform to the free spirit of Jewish life in America. This too is an anachronism. There are basic but deeply emotional differences, not fancied or idle, within the Jewish community. These should be accepted for the deeps they are and not as soulless items to be manipulated any more than we would decide a man's religion by majority vote. To some Jews, their beliefs on secular matters have all the untouchability of a religious conviction.

There is need to understand what voluntary cooperation really is or can be. We speak of it, and yet fail to recognize what it fully implies or is capable of. Cooperation is itself a program and a job. It requires patience. The adoption of something less than a distant ultimate goal is a useful study in patience. The tragic breakup of NCRAC was the result of impatience. It existed for eight years; and in eighty minutes lost its claim as a unifying factor in Jewish life. This because it insisted on preemptory action by majority vote, because it did not have the patience to keep open the avenue of communication and negotiation—its very reason for existence.

There are no perfect answers. I merely suggest that beyond the disparities and differences in Jewish life, yet containing them all in an embrace of solidarity, are the common bonds of Jewishness. Whatever the centrifugal forces, there remains the inexplicable, indefinable, but nonetheless real and overriding sense of common interest which Jews have as Jews. *This* is our unity. It is a unity that is always beyond the horizon. And a unity beyond controversy.

# (3)

## Education for What?

Of all of the problems in Jewish community life to which there are no easy answers, that of Jewish education presents perhaps the greatest difficulties. In most others we know with some completeness and even precision what the questions are to which answers, easy or difficult, must be found. We know that out of a sense of our historic traditional commitment to good works we must be of help to those in need, especially to those Jews abroad upon whom history has for so long laid so heavy a hand. We know that we must help rebuild Jewish communities destroyed by war or disaster. We feel that we must give explicit evidence of our deep feelings for the continued independence and security of the State of Israel. We know, too, that here in the United States we must maintain the community's religious, philanthropic and other institutions. Because we know the questions we have some idea of the answers. We at least know what they must embody. And we find that in most cases we can, little by little, cope with technical, organizational, and procedural difficulties.

We are not as clear about Jewish education because there is no consensus as to what Jewish education is to be for: what kind or kinds of American Jew we hope to have emerge in the generations ahead for whom an appropriate educational pattern, or several such, can be intelligently devised.

Generations ago in the lands to which the vast majority of American Jews trace their origin, the answer was easy—because there was really no deeply troubling question. Or because the conclusion was almost viscerally presumed and absorbed in the very bloodstream of every Jew: Jewish education was to make possible the life of a full Jew in a dominantly Jewish milieu or civilization.

For in Eastern Europe, even for scores of decades after the historic event known as the Emancipation of the Jews—at least on paper—in the Western World, Jews continued to live pretty much as insulated as in the ghettos of the Middle Ages. The Jewish youngster was educated and trained for what was, to all intents and purposes, a closed society of Jews in which he found his many challenges and his satisfactions. To study "God's Torah" was the cradle song crooned by every Jewish mother of every Jewish family, rich or poor, highly placed or humble, learned or ignorant. The hope for every Jewish child, certainly for the male child, was that he acquire the equipment and training in the religion of his ancestors that would place him solidly into his niche of a full, exclusive Jewish life. Outside, worldly, sectarian knowledge was halfheartedly, even grudgingly, acquired and, in the main, only to the extent necessary for the individual to earn his living. Thus, the goal of Jewish education was clear and pretty much instinctive: it was to shape a Jew for his own civilization, a Jew who could live fully and completely, without division of sentiment, in a life *apart* from the non-Jewish world.

A troubled atmosphere of change developed in this artificially sustained microcosm, a change that began to emerge and expand under the impact of a world-wide revolutionary transition. Some Jews began to think in terms of living as *part of,* not *apart from* the surrounding world; and this trend received its greatest thrust and momentum from the very earliest days of the United States— a country where Jews came to reside in greatest number and in which the national atmosphere was congenial and even inviting for a nonrestricted participation by all of its peoples. To an extent, this was operative, too, in some of the Western European countries.

In time, particularly here in the United States, Jews overwhelmingly chose to be part of, not apart from their environmental community, city and nation. Under the influence of strong, external, liberating and heady forces—and out of choice—Jews were set to abandon individual and group lives lived in isolation. They ceased to be only or exclusively Jews. They chose to live in multiple civilizations, to become integrated parts of the nations in which they lived and of the emerging international human family. Except for small fringes who believed they could still live as Jews did in the medieval Jewish ghetto and who were ready to be imbedded in the amber of an autarchic Polish, Lithuanian, or Ukrainian *shtetl* or its ersatz in the United States, Jews felt themselves to be an inherent part of a throbbing, if deeply troubled, world into which they strove harmoniously to fit their unique distinctiveness and values as Jews.

The era of Jews maintaining themselves as an insulated oddity has gone. Not even in Israel, called a Jewish state because it is the only one in which they are the majority of the people, can a Jew live what is casually thought of as a "completely" Jewish life. He must also lead an Israeli life. And this is so not only because of the demands of modern technology and the highly mechanized elements of our civilization. Other compelling forces are ponderous enough to turn the Israeli Jew away from an all-Jewish mooring. If he is a responsible citizen of Israel, he weighs his actions in terms of his Jewish background *and* of the requirements of his citizenship in the State of Israel. He cannot, as a responsible Israeli, speak out, solely by his Jewish tradition, against the racism of the Union of South Africa because of the importance of that country for the political and diplomatic support of the State of Israel. He cannot let his Jewish religious ethos strike out instinctively against what is happening in Communist Russia because he also nurses the hope that by a prudent denial of this self-expression he may help open the way for the migration of Soviet Jews to Israel.

So it is with other broad national and international developments. However the Israeli Jew's religious ethos and tradition may direct him to sympathy for a free and independent Algeria, he must be conscious of the political, economic, and military friendship demonstrated for Israel by the Republic of France. He cannot, as in the Suez episode, manifest his instinctive concern and compassion for the Jews of Egypt when his own Israeli state is threatened by border raids and by a military build-up for assault upon his country.

So with American Jews.

Living in a pluralistic society, the questions as to what are their desirable designs for living in which Jewish education can play its assigned role are both insistent and complex.

We have by this time assembled a good deal of revealing sociological information as to the extent and depth of the prevailing processes of Jewish education. It is enough to demonstrate that for the most part such education is pathetically limited in extent and of only a gossamer-thread thinness. At the same time, there is the ever-widening awareness that in the United States the enduring, acceptable differentiations are those deriving from our many religious heritages and cultures. The Irish American, the Italian American, the German American, the Polish American, gradually, over a period of generations, lets slip the qualifying Old World adjective. He ends up by becoming, if the link is at all remembered or retained, an American of Irish or German or Italian or Polish "descent." And as time goes on, even that thread loses its separatist coloration. But Americans have persevered in clinging to their religious differentiations. The religious identity and label are an accepted part of our society.

What then is to be our Jewish educational projection?

We can see that it needs and must have religion as its base or centrality. We can also conclude that, as has been true of Judaism throughout its history, it will make its adaptations and adjustments necessary for survival. We can also agree—we could not alter it if we would—that it must acquire and sustain a distinctive native character, asserting its own independence. It cannot be a colony or religious satellite of any other land, whether prewar Lithuania, Eastern Europe, or modern Israel. It must acquire a character of its own. It must discover a meaning of its own. And it must be in harmony with the free society in which we live.

We have some revealing information about the present state of Jewish education. This comes from the seven-year study, "Report on Jewish Education in the United States," prepared by Dr. Alexander M. Dushkin and Dr. Uriah Z. Engelman, that included a survey of thirty-three major American Jewish communities. This quarter-of-a-million-dollar study summed up its findings in the classic phrase of Mark Twain: American Jewish education "is a mile wide and an inch deep." One conclusion of the report, as given by Dr. Dushkin, is that in spite of the remarkable achievement of American Jewry in meeting many of the extraordinary and historic challenges to this generation of Jews, "the conditions prevailing in American Jewish education have often made for a Jewish shallowness and know-nothingism."

We now spend some sixty million dollars a year on elementary and secondary Jewish schooling. This is an increase of 230 per cent over 1947 costs. However, the organized communities provide only some 8 per cent of this money. Half of the total funds comes from the parents themselves. The rest is raised by the congregations which sponsor the schools. The Jewish community has not put Jewish education on the same wide, publicly supported basis as it has its overseas institutions, its civic defense organizations, and its communal interests such as its hospitals and its social services. It appears that nine of every ten Jewish youngsters are, at some time in their pre-teen years, enrolled in some kind of formal Jewish schooling. But the duration of their schooling is so brief—an average of three to four years—that, at best, only one-half of the group is enrolled at any one time. This is still a sizable number, estimated to be nearly 555,000, an increase in enrollment of more than

130 per cent in a decade. The more revealing statistic, however, is that only some 10 per cent of the students are getting a reasonably thorough education. Ninety per cent have a smattering of Jewish knowledge transmitted to them, with half of that number restricted to courses only during Sunday school sessions. Many schools have under one hundred pupils, with poor housing, inadequate facilities and meagerly trained teachers. Indeed, one teacher out of ten in the Sunday schools has himself had no formal Jewish schooling. Small and poorly financed, these congregational schools cannot meet the most modestly decent standards of pedagogical skill and of school management and administration.

Furthermore, the training is, for the most part, remote from the influence of home and parent. Indeed, most parents treat the school process as a vicarious atonement, not too deeply felt, for their own alienation from Jewishness. The study reveals that one parent out of four of those who readily pay for their children's religious training cannot name a single subject in the educational curricula.

There is, as a result, both a quantitative and a qualitative weakness which shows up most sharply in the failure of most Jewish children to pursue their Jewish schooling beyond the year of their Bar Mitzvah or confirmation. Except for all-day school pupils (the Yeshiva students), only about 3 per cent of the others continue with some form of formal Jewish education beyond the early teen-age years. "Our problem," says the Dushkin-Engelman survey, "is no longer that of getting our children to Jewish schools but rather of having them stay in the schools long enough to make this education valuable." The results of this imbalance are demonstrable.

Several years ago, the B'nai B'rith Hillel Foundations completed a study of Jewish students on three college campuses, an Ivy League school, a mid-Atlantic college, and a midwestern university. The four-year study provided for a periodic testing of Jewish knowledge and attitudes of the Jewish students who had entered school as freshmen in 1954 and who were graduated in 1958. This was a striking finding: while, unlike their parents' generation, most students affirmed their Jewish consciousness and did so more emphatically toward the end of their senior year than when they first entered school, there was "a shattering amount of Jewish illiteracy among youth."

Thousands of Jewish students—many, perhaps most, with high scholastic and intellectual equipment—come to college with dwarfed Jewish concepts. Thrust into the mature intellectual challenge of college study, their religious notions, arrested in childhood, are shaken in what Dr. Alfred Jospe, who directed the Hillel study, felicitously described as "a collision between Genesis and genetics." The Hillel director at one of the universities, who also serves on the faculty, reported: "As a teacher of freshmen I know what a shock it is to their ideas and values to meet the Greek mind of Periclean Athens in juxtaposition with the rabbinic mind of the Sunday school. The first impulse is to jettison the rabbinic system." Curiously, four years on the campus make many Jewish students more affirmative in their Jewishness but they are still left without an anchor in a solid knowledge of what that means. "Jewish students may be able to tell you little of their Jewish heritage but they know it exists. They understand that it may have a claim upon them and this they will usually not reject," said Dr. Jospe.

This conclusion—and we find similar ones in other studies—tells us that our shortcomings in formal Jewish education do not spring from an escapist youth but from an adult community that is blundering in its confusions.

Is the growing phenomenon of Jewish all-day schools an answer? Particularly among the Orthodox there has been a considerable growth of these schools, with the inevitable result that the Conservative and Reform Jews are also experimenting with this method. The total current enrollment in all-day schools is estimated to be some forty thousand—a striking increase over the enrollments of recent years but still a small proportion of those receiving any measure of Jewish education at all. This development reflects a rebellion against the inadequate, dismal education obtainable in the present afternoon school and Sunday classes, although day school parents, it has been pointed out, are diverse in their motives. If a broad impetus derives from a desire to provide the children with a sounder Jewish education, there is also the spur that the neighboring public schools are often unattractive.

From all evidence, the emphasis on Jewish education at all-day schools does not reduce the general scholastic interests and achievements. On the contrary, a disproportionate number of the high school graduates of these schools obtain state and other scholarships. Apparently secular education helps Jewish education and vice versa.

Yet there are other facets, and questions, not easily answered. Is the day school the only means to assure a high quality of Jewish education? Or does it isolate the Jewish youngster and indoctrinate instead of teach? Does it contribute to a weakening of the deeply imbedded American principle of a common public school education for all?

These considerations can be speculated on infinitely and I am not raising them in order to cast the slightest doubt as to the place of all-day schools in the total scheme of things. Indeed, I am all in favor of them—*for those who want them.* Nevertheless, even the most ardent advocates of the Jewish day school must concede that it does not provide the answer for the larger numbers of American Jews.

It may be that in this involuted life process, any proposed solution can only be a partial one. Perhaps there is no fixed answer. Certainly the compelling varieties of our Jewish lives caution us to be particularly wary and skeptical of absolutes. No formula can be satisfactory for a large group that is still in the midst of its evolution and Jewish life manifests itself most strikingly when its door is propped open to all influences.

Where a distinct, if limited, purpose is clearly foreseen, the machinery of Jewish education can be adjusted to suit.

For those who want to be Jewish specialists—rabbis, cantors, or even social workers—there are, with some adequacy, the educational instruments for their achievement. This is true for the aspiring Jewish scholar as well. For those who may choose to lead as nearly as possible a culturally-restricted Jewish life there are the Yeshivas to suit. Their pattern of life as Jews is like that of the Amish, one essentially apart from their environmental world.

I respect both the Amish and the products of the Lubavitcher Yeshivas for their qualities of uncompromising persistence, their defiant courage, their readiness to sacrifice the material values that hawk their temptations all around them. Our society would be much the poorer without them.

But for most of us there still remains the nagging problem: how shall our more modest lives be shaped, influenced, directed, trained? For the average American Jew, concerned with his children and eager to nourish their Jewish identity, these special answers are no answers at all. He must still grope for some aid toward the form of life that he has chosen as an American, at home in its history, culture, tradition and institutions, and yet, at the same time, disposed to be part of and to carry on the Jewish tradition. For those of us—that is, for most of us—it is futile to advocate that we become other than we are in our deepest inner impulses and convictions. We can only be helped as these are unimpaired and as we are guided toward a practice and a way of life that will not exact an excessive price for the multiple heritages and loyalties that are part of us and that we admire and want to sustain.

One of many possible answers—and as an alternative to weak congregational schools—is a wider development of community-wide schools financially supported by the community and conducted with respectful regard for all of the elements of the community. The ideological and theological differences that may have their place at a later stage in Jewish education apply with little force to such elementary subjects as the early study of the Bible, Jewish history, Hebrew or current events. For Jewish youth of all backgrounds to acquire their *aleph bet* together would, it seems to me, be the mildest of compromises. Indeed, in the limited years of schooling that they now get, most Jewish pupils never reach that stage of educational development that would enable them to choose with some rational clarity between the present divisions of Orthodoxy, Conservative and Reform.

The concept is hardly new. But since the eclipse of the Orthodox-steeped Talmud Torah that once was tucked into a dingy cranny of the old East Side, and the slow fading of the secular-oriented

Yiddish school, the move has been toward congregational control of Jewish schooling, and the community-wide school is the exception to the general trend.

Yet some of the exceptions are noteworthy; as, for example, the Minneapolis Talmud Torah. Half of this institution's budget comes from the Jewish federation of that city. By marshalling and coordinating its educational resources, Minneapolis has been able to provide physical facilities, a curriculum, a faculty, a sense of sustaining interest and a level of learning well beyond the average. The Minneapolis Talmud Torah is not without its detractors; some object to its monolithic dominance which allows little room for other types of Jewish schools, still others are concerned with the logistical difficulties a five-day curriculum imposes on suburban Jewish families. But, all in all, the superiority of the Minneapolis plan to what exists in most Jewish communities of like size has been demonstrated in the several generations of its existence.

The persuasive virtue of the community school is that it places the responsibility for an adequate program of Jewish education where it best belongs—squarely on the shoulders of the entire organized community. This is, at least under present circumstances, the speediest and sturdiest way to the kind of community enthusiasm and resources that Jewish education needs to lift it from its morass.

The most effective force to compel a move in this direction would be the rabbinate. Here again, the rabbis are called upon to put aside interdenominational differences and rivalries, without real injury to their theological beliefs, for the sake of an improved Jewish schooling. I can understand—if I cannot agree with—the unyielding objections of the minority: the Reform rabbi who will not compromise what he holds to be a firm religious principle and agree that Reform pupils attend class wearing *yarmalkes* as a concession to Orthodox pupils, or the Orthodox rabbi who insists that the study of Hebrew be focused only on the teaching of sacred studies and the ritual of *davening* (prayer). For these, there must be freedom to pursue Jewish education in their own way. But strict denominationalism is hardly the attitude of the Jewish community. The Dushkin-Engelman study tells us that few Jewish parents—

about one in ten—choose a religious school on an ideological basis. The denominational form plays little role in the parents' thinking about Jewish education or in their choice of a religious school for their children. The dominant factors are convenience, personalities and the educational reputation of the school.

## 2.

Other, less formalized forces have a role in Jewish education: adult education, a new enterprise in American Jewish life that is like a sprawling tent, giving cover to a variety of programs marked by diversity in motivation, approach, method, sponsorship and ultimate objectives; and the work of the non-synagogue-affiliated youth groups such as the B'nai B'rith Youth Organization.

In youth work, too, as in every organized expression of human interest, rivalries make their appearance, competitions and even power struggles that would seem unthinkable in what is so frail a plant as Jewish education in the United States. One example of this futile and bewildering conflict came to my attention when a regional gathering of the BBYO scheduled to be held during the period of the Purim holiday was called off as a result of opposition from the local rabbis. The youth program was planned as a week-long event in the atmosphere of a retreat with provision for special religious services as well as for lectures and discussion groups. It promised to be a week of singular dedication, offering much beyond what is available at a routine synagogue Purim observance. It was cancelled; and the local holiday services that were thereby "saved" from this "competitive" program proceeded with their usual pitifully sparse attendance.

Dr. Max F. Baer, the national director of the B'nai B'rith Youth Organization, in an analysis of the problem, wrote:

During the past several years we have witnessed an increasing number of conflicts between synagogues and Jewish youth organizations which are not part of the synagogues.

Concerned over sparse attendance at religious functions in the new and spacious synagogues, some rabbis feel threatened by successful religious programs conducted outside of the synagogues by youth-serving organizations.

Many synagogues which once made their meeting facilities available to local chapters of national Jewish youth groups now insist upon reserving this space for congregational youth clubs.

And he concluded:

It is not likely that more than a third of the Jewish youth in North America is affiliated with any kind of Jewish youth organization, local or national. Therefore, the real challenge is not so much one of competition among the different organizations nor one of duplication, but rather that of providing the additional resources required to motivate and recruit the many thousands of Jewish youngsters who are now deprived or who deprive themselves of the opportunities of a supervised Jewish group life. The desire on the part of the synagogues to sponsor youth groups which further their own ideologies is understandable. At the same time, if we are not to have a future Jewish community which is hopelessly splinterized and fragmentized, it is essential that Jewish youth also be encouraged to form groups in which they may learn to live with those who have differing concepts of Judaism and in which they can listen to varying points of view.

If our educational weaknesses are in great measure traceable to what is deemed to be a "lost generation," one that discovered its Jewishness from external events but that is illiterate in its Jewishness, one road back to an informed, educated and urbane Jewish community—a road that most needs repaving and restoring—is the road that will bring our rabbis, spiritual forces and educators to the Jewish adult. The wide cultural interests are there; Jews are notorious for their strivings for culture. They are book and "class" magazine buyers and readers; they form a high proportion of the audiences at concerts, operas, lectures, ballets. They are inquisitive and inveterate travelers abroad. By and large they have a higher degree of education than the general average. And they—we— now have the inestimable asset of increasing leisure time.

These are realities that can be put to good purpose. The learning process is not merely a teen-age adventure. The adult who expresses his interest in Jewish education vicariously—through his children —is no salvation for a community where adults, not youth, are the leadership and power structure. To transfer the problem of Jewish illiteracy to the next generation is the sad experience of an adult generation defaulting on itself, on its own maturing, as well as on its responsibilities to the succeeding generation.

The new receptivity to Judaism and things Jewish that is stirring in American Jewish life is mirrored in the recent developments and expansions in adult Jewish study. True, it is still a fringe activity, a hit-or-miss proposition lacking real standards and reaching on a sustained basis, at most, some 5 per cent of the available adults, so that the real potential remains unreached and untouched. Educators in this field are still uncertain as to methods that can stress *active* participation, as against the passive learning process, that is needed as an incentive for the adult student. And there is the underlying problem of adult education's marginal status in the community, way down on any list of priorities, notwithstanding its values and high potential.

Still, the interest is there, and it is burgeoning. I have seen the intensity and the joy with which "students" have joined in institutes of adult Jewish education—the secluded and restful retreat for study and discussion that is a modern approach to the Babylonian *kallah.* And in many scattered communities, rabbis and educators have conducted some imaginative and effective study programs that carry their own built-in incentives for the adults they reach.

In all of this, it seems to me, our rabbis and pedagogical experts can be effective and can direct some strong and noble efforts. Of course the task will not be easy, but how stimulating the aspiration. "Our grasp," as the poet said, "must exceed our reach or what's a heaven for?" Such an approach—reaching the Jewish child through his adults—is to take a new look at the possibilities with adults, with parents, and to create through them a family atmosphere out of which there will naturally grow the impulses for a meaningful Jewish expression in all our lives. Given that as a goal, the techniques and procedures will in due course be developed. And there will, no doubt, be many of them, different in approach and emphasis, but with a goal in common.

There is a Jewish press, now struggling against community indifference and its own inadequacies. It should be better; and it can be, just as it can be directed to a more useful and important place in Jewish adult and youth education. We need truly independent journals, free to probe, to analyze, to reveal—above all, to raise our intellectual sights. We need not abandon the ideal of an American Jewish journalism as good and better than the high quality of the *London Jewish Chronicle*. We need also to be steered away from the shallow and the superficial in what now is prevalent in Jewish informational literature and apologetics. We certainly need help in immunization against the deceptive lures of sloganeering in Jewish life. We need to respond to Solomon Shechter's advice that "Judaism need not be advertised; it needs to be taught."

Finally, there is perhaps another guiding signpost to be found in a fuller exploration and intensification of the tradition of "service" that looms as so large a part of the Jewish heritage and that so increasingly marks the contemporary American Jew. In this, formal knowledge has its part; but understanding and depth of compassion have even more of a part to play. Literature has its place: as a human outcry rather than as the scholastic's study of an ancient language or, for that matter, rather than as a modern Berlitz conversation medium. Religion has its place, of which "good works" is, in our environment, its most honored expression. The synagogue has its place—as catalyst and as fountainhead but not as monopolist.

Strengthening the tradition of service takes into account the demonstrated and considerable urge among Jews for public service and for group participation, an urge that needs only be encouraged, directed and honored by its achievements. For in a survival that is to be creative and soul-satisfying, Jewish education must be far, far more than an acquisitive process of hoarding dates and facts. It must be so structured as to be capable of generative capacities.

And since human and civic service is to so large an extent an imitative process, its roots must be planted in the home. Only as there is a Jewish home in which Jewish (and all human) causes are a natural, native interest and expression, in which consideration of Jewish affairs is a normal part of the give-and-take of the family circle, can we hope to broaden and make meaningful, for the far larger Jewish youth than is included in the present school enrollment, an alert awareness of Jewishness and a responsiveness to it.

Perhaps we can achieve our best *effect* by countering our greatest *defect:* the home where Jewishness is something peripheral and external. You *go* to the synagogue, you *go* to the center, you *go* to a meeting on anti-Semitism, always a going out; far too rarely is there a gathering in. To modify this prevalent experience calls for a new look, a process more serious than has yet been made to determine where the Jewish adult comes in, how his education can be resumed and how it must be sustained throughout his life. We may induce more questions than we have answers for. But there is a profound wisdom in the asking of important questions, even though we may have a long wait for the right answers.

For out of such adults, Jewish families absorbed in their intellectual growth, there will come vitality enough, widely expressed and as varied and as enriching as our pluralistic culture invites us to create.

The expanding enlistment of such families will inevitably enable them to find many suitable ways for sustaining the process of Jewish education.

And a growing community of such families will by itself be our best assurance for Jewish continuity.

# (4)

## *A Place in the Sun*

Every living Jew and every Jew still to be born will bear in his historic memories a welt-mark of the whiplash that divides what preceded and what followed the advent of Adolf Hitler and Nazism.

Jewish history is not unfamiliar with persecution. The dispersion of the Jews after the Second Commonwealth has been marked by, at the mildest, a series of disabilities and, at the worst, severe repression, inquisitorial torments, and bloodstained mob rampage, as in the many decades of the Crusades.

In my youth I was embittered by the knowledge of the pogrom waves in Russia. That was a time when the world was horrified by reports of those maimed and killed as a result of Czarist-inspired agitation. Especially significant in modern history was the terror outbreak in Russia which culminated in the revolting, obscene attacks in Kishinev in April 1903. With its forty-five killed and eighty-six wounded and crippled, Kishinev came to have a macabre meaning for its time—like and yet how unlike—Dachau and Auschwitz of forty years later.

This pre-World War I mob savagery was put down as the misdeeds of a still semi-barbaric Russian people. The earlier history of anti-Jewish outbreaks was attributed to the long-prevailing religious fanticism (there was for the Christian world the Hundred Years War of Protestants and Catholics). And there were always bigots and warped minds that could derive satisfaction from watching the hurts of others.

Hitlerism introduced something new: an unparalleled brutality and satanism that became a fermenting force in world affairs. In Hitler's hands anti-Semitism was a political weapon, a tool of conquest first of the German people and later, as an article of export, for further conquests abroad. It ended up in a stunned realization by his victims, and by the world at large. As Hannah Arendt has so brilliantly put it: "The tragedy of our time has been that only the emergence of crimes unknown in quality and proportion and not foreseen by the Ten Commandments made us realize . . . that the whole of nearly 3,000 years of Western civilization . . . with all its implied beliefs, traditions, standards of judgment, has come toppling down over our heads."

My early memories of anti-Semitism in the United States are of small episodes. In those years, American Jews—so benign was the world—were troubled, for example, by anti-Semitic stereotypes on the vaudeville stage. The first important efforts to contend with such slurs and defamations of the Jews were organized at about the time I was born, although there had been some earlier, transient attempts to cope with actions that wounded Jewish dignity and that stained the image of the American Jew. There was distress at offensive jokes about Jews and of caricatures that invariably projected the long hooked nose, dangling sleeves, and loosely-tied trousers of the misfit. There was great rejoicing when we heard of successful efforts that effected the expunging of offensive lines from a play or the moderation of a comic's caricature of Jews.

For all of their comparative mildness, the experiences were still galling. The lampooning hurt us deep down, even if we did not foresee its natural links to the later Nazi blood baths, or failed to project the sportive ridicule of one group of mankind into what it was: an early step in a decline to world ignominy. There is, for every member of a minority group, a sensitive area for which he alone is the qualified diagnostician. *He* knows how raw is the wound inflicted on self-respect; *he* knows how it strangles the normal strivings of every man for his individual human dignity.

Still, in the early years of the century, this seemed to be the direct experience (apart from revolting reports from inside Russia), along with shrugged-off affronts on the social level, the stance of a self-styled superior caste that was plainly in decay and that thought to hold back the inevitable by practicing its exclusory form of social snobbery.

A change from the deceptive comparative serenity took place shortly after World War I. There was the wide circulation of the fraudulent "Protocols of the Elders of Zion." There was the emergence all over the United States of the Ku Klux Klan—Jew-baiting, Catholic-baiting, Negro-baiting, alien-baiting. There were the fulminations of the discredited and later disowned *Dearborn Independent.*

I myself saw the Klan crosses burn. I lived in Missouri in the 1920's and for a brief interval went to school at Lawrence, Kansas. The flaming torch—a perversion of what was preached as a symbol of universal love and brotherhood—was an upsetting experience. Even then it did not take on for me the depth of meaning and fear that it did for immigrant Jews who could recall from their ghetto memories experiences of pogroms and personal indignities that were almost a normal part of the daily lives of the Jews of Russia.

But there was still a difference between the anti-Semitism that showed itself in the United States and the anti-Semitism that had its seedbed in racist Germany. Here, in our own country, the general experience was for the anti-Semite to *deny* that he was one. He was only, he whined, against "bad" Jews. He did not dare

reveal himself as rejecting the deeply ingrained American ethic of
fair play for everyone. Even a later, outspoken Coughlin was
careful to adumbrate that he was really a friend of the Jews,
*but.* . . . This was a climate different from that prevailing in
Germany, where folk traditions running back many, many centuries were daubed with the infamy of persecution and hatred,
where the nation's most shining historic personalities were marked
with bigoted fanaticism, where, if you mistakenly described a man
as a friend of the Jews, he would like as not challenge you to a
duel.

In our own country, even a Ku Klux Klan meeting began with a
pledge of allegiance to an America whose charter of Independence
spoke of all men as being created equal.

To a young man without knowledge of the dark satanic subconscious that can exert so crushing an influence on the individual
and even more on the mob, it was of course unpleasant, but not
intolerable. There was even an inverted vanity in being singled
out for such widespread attention.

But this was before Hitler—before the gas chambers and ovens
for six million Jews, before the uprooting of millions of Jews from
their many national homes and cultures throughout Europe of
which they were so extraordinary an adornment. Can I—can any
Jew—ever blot out from mind the barely alive skeletons, the glazed
eyes of despair, the hunted and haunted cringe of the almost flesh-
less bodies? It may be good shock therapy for the world to force
itself once a year to look upon this photographed record of horror,
to see these films and have a full measure of the hellish depths into
which man's capacity for hatred can tumble the entire world.

One outgrowth of this inferno of fire and torment was an
aroused American Jewry with more of the innate dignity for determined self-defense; with more sensitivity to the hurts to every and
any man; with better-financed and better-organized defense agencies; and, above all, with a wiser and less parochial outlook. The
lesson was learned the hard way: it was not just anti-Semitism that
was to be contended with; there was a more vital world duel be-

tween those who wished dignity and decency for all men and those
who would enslave them or destroy them.

And we American Jews had an important part in that duel.

We were ashamed of our own past blindness and failures as
well as of the blindness and failures of Jewish communities that
have since that time been all but obliterated. Failure to foresee in
good time the dreadful scope of the racist menace and to repulse
it had proved all too tragically costly.

An old friend of mine, Morris D. Waldman, had some revealing
experiences to tell in his autobiographical book *Not By Power*. A
pioneer Jewish social service worker, he gave his last active years
to the service of the American Jewish Committee, of which he was
chief executive in the thirties and forties. In this capacity he visited
Germany in 1930, before the full blood-drama of Hitler was en-
acted. In the fall of that year, he reported on what he saw in the
growing Nazi menace in Germany before a meeting of his organization that was augmented by other, equally prominent Jewish
leaders. He told them in detail of the growing strength of the National Socialist movement and of those people in Germany not as
yet full members of the Party who were prepared to support its
doctrines. And he pleaded for a concerted effort to meet this immediate challenge to the Jews of Germany and of Europe and to
all decent and human values.

Even at that late date, Waldman tells, only a very few of the hundred leading American Jews who were at the meeting believed his
story. On the other hand, there were several who took him to task
for what they regarded as an unbalanced and pessimistic judgment. One man, the head of an important Jewish organization,
gave his view boldly from the platform, expressing the certainty
that the Nazis would never acquire governmental power and that
even if they did they would not dare put into force their shocking,
brazenly declared policies.

I, too, had that experience—much later and more directly from
within Germany itself. Prior to World War II, the most important
B'nai B'rith constituency outside of North America was among the
German Jews. As a young man, I was privileged to meet one who

was then and later its leader, the sainted Rabbi Leo Baeck. However, I had little contact with the problems of the German members of the B'nai B'rith until I became president of the international organization. It was then that I had to deal with the vast
claims pending against the West German Republic for the Nazi
confiscation of B'nai B'rith property. And I learned a good deal
during the almost six years of negotiation that ended, finally, with a
settlement of our claims on the eve of my last days in office. What
amazed me most was my discovery that, until the day of the confiscation in April 1937, the B'nai B'rith movement there went on
as if what *did* happen could not happen. Here were some of the
most cultured, most highly educated Jews of Germany, some fifteen thousand of them, who, despite what was all around them,
were set to try to continue business as usual.

I realize, of course, that it is easy and may perhaps do an injustice to be wise after the event. Even with a better insight into
what later transpired, what could the Jews of Germany have
done to stop Hitler?

But if neither the German Jews nor the world saw clearly enough
in the early days of Nazism, we can certainly *now* take note of the
very earliest revealing symptoms of this mass mania.

There were other consequences of Hitler and of his final hours
in the funeral pyres of a beleagured Berlin. The famous historian
Charles A. Beard has submitted as one of the great lessons of history that "the bee pollinates the flower that it robs."

So, too, with Germany, with the Jews, with the United States,
with Europe, and with all the world.

For Germany, there is left a wretched heritage. The German
people are still struggling with the problem of explaining to themselves and to an embittered and skeptical world what it was that
happened to this home of *Kultur* and culture. Above all, they are
faced with the formidable task of absorbing in their marrow the
vivid lesson of modern history: that the tyrant and the hater harm
not only the immediate victim but spread their deadly infection to
all who are drawn into their nauseous web.

For the Jews, wherever they lived, there followed a new sensitivity, a new dignity in an erect posture—and the miracle of the establishment of Israel.

For Europe there was the painfully acquired sense of the umbilical cord that links injustice for a group, however small, with debasement for all men.

In the United States there was a spreading awareness that prejudice and bigotry, when you get right down to it, are destructive to our natural heritage and purposes and that their manifestations, marked or superficial, must not be coddled if they are not to grow suddenly into an all-destructive juggernaut.

This awareness has, in a measure, reached out over the world as a whole. There is the realization that despotism, colonialism, and the chaining of one nationality or race by another are inevitable preludes to disaster, a blueprint for an Armageddon in which all civilization will perish. Only one blustering imperialism still extends its rapacious arms—the new Communist imperialism that has swallowed so many countries and peoples in Europe and in Asia. Yet I believe that a world that knew Hitlerism, saw its horrors and beat it into lifelessness, will take the measure of this apocalyptic beast as well.

Hitlerism has taught us all something vital even though we cannot quickly, and on all occasions, act decisively by its bitter lessons.

This is not to say that there are not residues of the Nazi stench. Some months ago I was in a Latin-American country where I discussed local instances of anti-Semitism in what is one of the freest countries in that part of the globe. I was horrified when an informed observer told me that "until the influx of refugees after the Hitler period, we really had no such problem here. This is a free country with high standards of human behavior. But since the Jewish population has grown by some 300 per cent, Hitler's ideas are being remembered and shadowy resentments are beginning to develop."

I learned something of the same order from an intelligent citizen of The Netherlands. His answer, too, sobered me and gave me much to think about. "Before Hitler," he said, "there was no problem. You would suppose that with the whole country suffering as it did, nothing would be left of the old anti-Semitic attitudes. Unfortunately, the human capacity to nurse resentment and distrust of one's neighbor and to employ hate as a self-sustaining balm is still all too prevalent. Hitler has left his imprint; the evidence of that print is still with us."

2.

For the American Jewish community the lessons of Hitler were particularly striking and vivid. There was, in the first place, the early counterreaction of a newly asserted self-dignity, a posture indispensable toward creative action. There was the refinement of our sensitivity. Out of our agonizing experiences, we came to be, for the world at large, a sensitized litmus paper reacting to the slightest drop of poison in the biological chemistry of a free society.

I had an experience with that some years ago. In the Near East I met with an American diplomat in pleasant conversations about a variety of matters. On one occasion he asked me to introduce him to the leading Jews of the community in the country in which he was stationed. I sounded him out as to why he wanted this and he explained very simply: his foreign service experiences had taught him that the Jews in a community seem to have the best premonition of lurking dangers.

Another consequence for the American Jewish community is that it set about to organize its defense program on a scale far broader and more effective than ever before. For this, sacrifice has been necessary, in money, in effort, in the inevitable confusion and crosscurrents of enlarged organization.

It also involved still another openly accepted risk—that of unpopularity. For it meant that the Jews, having seen the inevitable interrelationships, feel impelled to come to the rescue of other tormented, persecuted, or mistreated minorities rather than using them as lightning rods to deflect hostile attention from themselves. Thus a community of interests has matured into full flower. Every invasion of human rights is presumed by its very existence to be a threat to the Jews.

Against this background I foresee here in the United States one overriding issue, an issue that reaches down to the roots of the future character of American life. This issue is affecting millions who are non-Jews, but we know that in its inexorable way, it will touch, in greater or lesser measure, the lives of all within America's boundaries. Now and for years to come, we will have to meet the challenge of a reshaping of our own national life revolving around the school integration decision of the Supreme Court and of the onward march for real, not pretended, legal equality.

It has its many and many-faceted problems. But it is inescapably there to focus our attention on the whole depth and reach of the root subject of human rights. Its effective handling will demonstrate that we can meet the vital contemporary tests of our American democracy. Whatever we do will have world-wide implications. For already this subject is bringing out into the open long-restrained questions as to the quality of America's claim to the moral leadership of the free world.

Years ago, while in the service of our Government, I was struck by the importance, not to speak of the reality, of the heterogeneous character of the United States. I knew that it was easy to err when you were at a great distance from a community and from the people intimately affected by an important law and the social upheaval it may generate. I was never in doubt about the soundness of the principles involved in the Supreme Court's decision, nor of B'nai B'rith's responsibility to support these principles. I did, however, want to see for myself just what this particular issue meant to those who had to contend with the practical implementation of the Supreme Court decision. And so I went South, not to the border states, but to the Mississippi Delta. I traveled by automobile from one town to another and met morning, noon, and night with people from all walks of life in the Jewish community, at town crossroads, in private homes, and in public halls and synagogues and temples.

I took with me as part of my intellectual baggage the awareness that a response, even on the part of people who are firm in their devotion to the underlying ethical concepts of our Judaeo-Christian civilization, is still to be measured by the influence of their direct environment. I knew that it was easier to make a ringing speech on desegregation from a platform in Madison Square Garden, in the Chicago Stadium, or in the Cow Palace than in the Elks Club of a small town in Mississippi. My experiences led me to expect that the very same speaker, no matter how honest, will modify what he says depending on where he speaks—at the very least in emphasis and tone.

So I was not totally unprepared for the bitter words I heard against all of the national American Jewish organizations in the civic defense field. This, from my own coreligionists in Mississippi. Some insisted that they would have no problem at all if we could accept their conclusion that "it is no concern of the Jew." When I pointed out the obvious—that in his quest for equality, the American Jew can expect no more for himself than he is prepared to give to others in similar situations—the average and decent man's reply was to agree. "But don't be so loud or so active about it," he whispered to me.

There were those who stressed the statistical problem that made the difference for integration in the North and the South. They argued that many of the people affected were not ready for its full acceptance. Faced with the evidence that under the "separate but equal" doctrine they had done very little, their last desperate admonition was, "This is a problem that can only be solved by education, not by law."

Everyone seems to agree that education is indispensable in any massive effort to cope with prejudice. A deep-rooted prejudice cannot be legislated against effectively, nor erased by the verdict of a court. But a society's discrimination based on prejudice calls for a more far-reaching therapy. Both education and legislation have their place; and where the force of law is used too late, where discriminatory practices build their fortresses into the accepted ways of life, the operation of either education or legislation becomes far, far more difficult.

My experience in the Mississippi Delta was most informative. At times, it was exciting though disturbing to witness the clash of high conscience and prudent self-interest, the internal struggle of many good people.

Rarely did I hear from the Jews in the Delta or elsewhere in the South an expression of personal bitterness against the Negro. Now and then the NAACP came under attack, as did the Anti-Defamation League. There were frequent expressions of personal affection for the Negro, genuine though perhaps slightly condescending. Often I heard expressions of warm sympathy and most frequently a hope that the American Negro would someday come fully into his own. There was, in fact, a wonderfully humane approach, as far as the individual Negro was concerned.

What has all this to do with discrimination or prejudice against the Jew?

From the moment I set foot in Greenville, Mississippi, to the moment I left Jackson and went North, I heard, time and again: "You see, we enjoy equal status down here. Our families have lived here for several generations. We are accepted. We are members of boards of directors of banks, presidents of Rotary clubs and chambers of commerce. When B'nai B'rith, which is known as *the* Jewish organization down here, takes a leading part in this controversy our white non-Jewish neighbors are not so sure of us. You continue what you are doing and we will end up with a strong Ku Klux Klan, economic boycott, and everything else against the Jews in the South."

My standard observation, at this point, was to say: "Jewish organizations have taken no greater leadership in this than most of the Protestant and Catholic church groups and social welfare groups that are not Jewish. What about them?" And here the hollowness of the local claim revealed itself. The customary answer was either: "Well, they're not Jews," or, "After all, they're not in the minority."

Accepted? Equal status? How accurate were these claims? Or were they comfortable self-delusions? The tragedy was that all of these fine, good-intentioned, and kindly people did not relate the two situations. They would not see the historic truth that to deal with the Jewish position narrowly and selfishly gets us nowhere.

Some time after my trip to the Delta, I visited Montgomery, Alabama. Here I met with people from all over the state and we talked candidly behind closed doors.

What I heard in the old capital of the Confederacy was the same duality. If anything, Little Rock and the events that had transpired there had intensified inchoate feelings. One Alabama Jewish leader said at a large meeting that integration of the schools was inevitable, and claimed that he predicted this some time before the Supreme Court decision. But, he added, the Supreme Court decision had set back integration in Montgomery and elsewhere in the Deep South. Another outstanding citizen frankly admitted that he liked the "Southern way of life" and that he didn't like us at all for what we were "doing to it."

Both seemed to me to be begging the question. Both refused to face up to the fact that all human rights are parts of an organic total; that their corruption, here or there, is bound to affect all the others.

On this trip to Alabama I found the people in the midst of a primary campaign for state office. One of the candidates for governor was John G. Crommelin, a retired Navy admiral. Earlier, he had entered the race for senator against the popular incumbent Lister Hill, and, while he lost, had succeeded in getting a sizable vote. In the primary race for governor there were fourteen candidates and he was given little chance to win the Democratic nomination which in Alabama was tantamount to election.

In his senatorial campaign Crommelin had wallowed in anti-Semitic slogans. In his campaign for governor he completely threw caution to the winds. Some of his television speeches were as rabid as a Goebbels broadcast. And he pulled all the stops, blaming the Jews above all others for the integration fight.

Despite his poor political prospects, many Jews of Alabama were concerned and deeply unhappy about his vicious campaign. As a casual visitor at one meeting I heard some well-intentioned and able citizens express their concern that Northern pro-civil-rights groups or Jews from the North might join to "stop" Crommelin. Crommelin himself was not finicky about support from outside the State of Alabama. He was taking all the help he could get from professional anti-Semites and their behind-the-scenes patrons wherever they lived. I had to steady myself as I heard remarks reminiscent of the German period when Nazism seemed a passing fancy to so many Jews.

It *was* an Alabama political problem. It probably was good judgment to avoid the hue and cry of out-of-state interference, in view of a generally tense situation.

What finally moved me to speak was the claim that what happened in Alabama was of concern only to Alabama. Surely if Crommelin won high office, all America—and more—would be affected by the poison. I was saddened to see that a generation after the Nazi experience, there was still faith in geographical boundaries as barriers to hate and its inevitable aftermath.

There were conflicting views within the group on strategy: whether to ignore Crommelin or fight him, and, if so, how. But there was also overwhelming sentiment that whatever the strategy, it should be devised and carried out by those who lived in Alabama, without "interference" from the likes of me or any other visitor from the North.

I agreed. Certainly their concerns were more intimate and they had a better grasp of the local problems. But I also had to remind them that "you are not planning for yourselves alone. What you do, or fail to do, for the sake of your children's future in Alabama, can have just as much impact on my kids in Illinois."

My visits to the South taught me much about the need for a sympathetic understanding of the real-life complications that may follow our most high-minded resolves. At the same time, I went back home more than ever convinced of the corrosive influence of the idea of a "toleration" or apparent "acceptance" by the majority of the minority; indeed, of its disastrous void. The Southern Jews who consider themselves "accepted" and yet who find themselves discriminated against in a crisis situation do not seem to see the flimsy structure on which their immediate hopes rest; or that they are at best on a kind of continual probation. The appearance of equality may be there but the *fact* is not. And there is no greater danger in the eternal war for human dignity than the *illusion* of equality.

An American Jew *ha*s to be concerned with integration, just as he is concerned with anti-Semitism. Just as every minority must be concerned with anti-Semitism as with its own problems—and every living human being is, in several aspects of his life, one of a minority. Certainly we, the so-called "whites" of the world, are having that truth branded into our contemporary experiences.

The effective realization of human dignity where a minority group is concerned also calls for an internal, psychological decision. A group that fails to respect itself and to assert its rights, quietly, effectively and unostentatiously, will end up by finding them eroded. To accept—however imperceptibly—a second-class status, is to perpetuate it.

I recall that this problem was put to me in a question by a member of a youth group at a meeting in the summer of 1954. The answer I gave then is, I feel, as timely today.

"There is," I said, "little more un-American than the failure to question the position of any governmental agency if in your honest judgment that position is inimical to the interests of our country. This is true whether the position affects Israel or any other policy. The United States has committed itself, starting with Greece and Turkey, to a policy of support for any bastion of freedom wherever it might be, in order to extend and promote the maintenance of national independence against Communist expansion. When my country, through its Department of State, takes a position which in my judgment violates that sound principle, and it affects Israel, I see no reason for limiting my criticism to the quiet of a room and not to say what I have to say in front of an audience or in the presence of public officials.

". . . We who are Jews of America (and whose stake in the solutions of the problems affecting Israel is appreciated by most of our fellow Americans) cannot compromise in the discharge of our full obligations as American citizens. We need not be deterred by anyone who would caution us to keep quiet. Some people kept quiet twelve and twenty years ago during the Hitler period. When they wanted to speak, it was too late. Let us now, and in the generations to come, speak out early enough and clearly enough. Let us not be intimidated."

When a self-respecting minority foregoes its inalienable right to be heard, and thereby foregoes its rights, it not only scuttles its self-respect and weakens its own cause—it weakens, by that act, the very basis of democracy itself. When out of fear or intimidation decent Americans of whatever faith fail to express what they believe, the whole process of democracy loses vitality. Earnest and honest differences must be debated in a free society, if that society is to endure. The American Jew owes it to the America he loves to give the best of his thinking and to give his views full expression in those areas where he may be especially competent even though his interest may be unusually intimate. Accepting any other position means accepting voluntarily a limitation of the hallowed rights of American citizenship.

### 3.

This is a period of great struggle between conflicting ideologies in the universe. Some have attempted to enforce, during the period of the "cold war," limitations on American freedoms that may be justified only and momentarily in a period of a fighting war. In World War II Donald Nelson, then chief of war production, made a cogent statement which I have never forgotten. He said: "It would be a pity if, in our effort to save our way of life, we lost it. And if we must give up rights and freedoms which are traditionally American we must make certain that this is temporary."

There are people who shout the caution that the attack from without is so remorseless and powerful that we must follow by drawing a curtain on certain of the basic freedoms of American life. We have been witness to efforts to tamper with some of the ancient and sacred rights of citizenship—the Fifth Amendment for example—depicted by many as a refuge for traitors and racketeers.

Doubtless, some have taken advantage of the Fifth Amendment

to disguise or remain quiet about their treachery or crime. But our concept of justice rests on a more compelling thesis. And if we yield what distinguishes America—then what will the shooting war be all about?

We are by now far removed from the events that precipitated the birth of this nation, with the result that our growth as a nation, the extraordinary development of our economy, our luxuries and comforts have induced an amnesia as to the simple truths of the founding of the United States, the clarion call of its Declaration of Independence, the drafting of its Constitution and its Bill of Rights.

Our founding fathers understood the need for a law that protected the individual against self-incrimination. If we expect to enjoy human rights as a people, we cannot stand idly by and permit landmarks such as the Fifth Amendment to be undermined because some few exploit it for private benefit. The real issue is not on the transient benefits they obtain but on the consequence to our entire seamless fabric of justice.

The solid day-by-day underpinning of the rights of every American is made up of countless little acts by large numbers of people. Our struggle for universal moral concepts is of the essence in man's search for his own dignity. Assuming the rights and discharging the responsibilities that go with our democratic society can be each man's daily contribution to that struggle, which allows no room for the summer soldier or the sunshine patriot.

I have traveled in countries which are democracies only in form. I have found groups who feel no sense of identification with what happens in their community, province, state, or nation. They confine themselves to their own selfish, immediate, and narrow interests, and have no part in the essential process of democratic living.

This must not happen here.

Unless people are concerned with their neighborhood, their town, their state, and unless they are willing to take some time away from their own selfish concerns—to get out to vote, to clean up the streets, to learn about governmental process, to accept from time to time official responsibility, to work on committees, to maintain contacts with government at its various levels, to concern themselves with school, fire, and police departments— unless these things are actively done by more and more people, then whatever the rights are that man is alleged to enjoy in a free country, they will deteriorate and may ultimately disappear.

Some groups seem to delight in treating, or even attacking, the government or its agencies as if they were not flesh of our flesh. Our freedom, our government is, in a country like the United States, what *we* make it. It is not something apart from us—it is *us.* The Congress more nearly approximates what the people want than most of us realize. Legislation without vision is not the fault of Congress as much as it is the consequence of the failure of citizens to be informed on the issues.

The struggle to "secure these rights," as projected by our Declaration of Independence, must go on, but its forms change before our very eyes. More and more, the special tactics of the agencies created by the American Jewish community are merging with those of non-Jewish agencies of like character. More and more, the realization that the hurt of one is the hurt of all is possessing the leadership in this field of human endeavor.

There is still another aspect of this entire problem which is a strong element in my faith as an American Jew. In Dr. Mordecai Kaplan's *Judaism as a Civilization,* there is one observation of particular cogency. He deplores that Jews are inclined to think of their position too frequently in terms of what others say or do about us. Anti-Semitism is a favorite topic and, as he pointed out, much of Jewish life concerns itself with the effect of this phenomena on Jews.

In the final analysis the best answer to anti-Semitism is a positive and affirmative self-respect and our full participation in the broader struggle for human rights. Chasing bigots and transgressors of human dignity in and out of their ratholes is a job that needs to be done. But it is not the answer.

For the American Jew the answer is to strengthen his religious commitments, bring greater meaning to the educational processes for youth and adult alike, and become more creative in our synthesis of old culture with new. If, at the same time, American Jewry participates with whole heart in the struggle for human dignity for all, we will have the best answer to the more basic question as to the kind of world in which we need not shield Jews from anti-Semitism.

The cynic posing as the realist concludes that "there will always be anti-Semitism," thereby unconsciously revealing also his optimism that there will always be Jews. He draws on history and its long succession of anti-Jewish excesses—as if history can be probed without its comparatives and relationships. He sees Hitlerism solely in terms of its unquestioned monstrous madness. He does not see what else has followed.

But a stone thrown into a lake has many ripples.

I have watched the play and interplay of anti-Semitism and the natural reaction it evoked with horror, with agony of soul—and with wonder at man's capacity to rebuild upon ruins and to rescue an eternal flame from the underground in which it had been guttered out.

There was Hitler and the Nazism that he whelped. There is also the universal awareness of the cause-and-effect relationship of prejudice—and world-wide human disaster.

# (5)

## Big Money and Big Givers

1954 was a good year for Jewish rhetoric. American Jewry was three hundred years old. The commemorative voices were not to be denied their moments of exaltation. From podium and pulpit orators contested with their splendid words. The three centuries of Jewish life in a democratic milieu were wreathed in paean, dramatized, memorialized, and exalted, by a community affirming pride in its past and confident of a robust future.

In this abundant talk, along with remembering the intrepid twenty-three Jews who first arrived in Nieuw Amsterdam in 1654, the most popular tercentenary theme was that flourishing symbol of Jewish life—*philanthropy*.

American Jews are generous givers. Their benevolence is rooted in the tradition of *Gemilat chasadim* (deeds of loving-kindness). The statistics of what they pour out for sweet charity's sake tell the story of a community secure in its freedoms, grateful for its prosperity, and responsive, with a religious intensity, to the calls for benevolence. Out of all this has come an industry, organized fund raising, now grown to vast proportions.

"The payment of a regular contribution," suggests historian Salo Baron, "may indeed become the dominant new form of community allegiance." Jewish philanthropy is big business, highly professionalized and marked by the manipulative skills of Madison Avenue salesmanship.

Precise figures of Jewish benevolence are difficult to determine. A conservative estimate is that American Jews give about $200,-000,000 annually for Jewish causes alone. This is twenty times what it was thirty-five years ago, in contrast to a Jewish population growth of less than one-fifth. In the process, fund raising has become a catalyst, the measure of conscience and the *esprit de corps* of organized Jewish life.*

In total dollar terms the American community is the most liberal, openhanded Jewish group in the world. American Jews give more —by virtue of having more to give. Yet an analysis based on population percentages or per capita wealth (and this is without apology for American Jewry, whose generosity needs none) would modify this picture. South African communities might show up as bigger givers, in percentage terms. Unlike the sprawling, heterogeneous American Jewry, the South African Jews live in small and cohesive enclaves and have a closer and more direct knowledge of their internal needs and affairs. This leads to more equitable as well as to higher levels of giving.

Swiss Jewry may consider its generosity negligible by contrast with the enormous American abundance; but it claims that, on the basis of individual incomes, its wealthier members are more

---

* This does not include markedly generous support by Jews of non-Jewish and nonsectarian appeals. Nor does it account for membership fees to Jewish organizations and synagogues, tuition to Jewish educational institutions, or similar expenditures which are also part of community financing.

generous than the big givers of American Jewry. British Jews, lacking the tax-deduction advantages Americans enjoy, can claim that by out-of-pocket criteria the British Jewish ratio of giving is higher.

Still another insight follows from every attempt to measure American Jewry's philanthropy against the statistics of the community's economic growth. There are some grounds for concluding that the present generation of American Jews does not match the liberality of its less affluent forefathers.

Yet the dollars-and-cents statistics of American Jewry's altruism are undeniably impressive. The American Jewish community has been, far and away, the major Jewish source of voluntary funds for refugees' relief and resettlement, for aid to Israel, and for other overseas needs. It has carried the massive burden of being its brother's keeper for Jews in other lands, while raising more than one hundred million dollars a year to finance its own domestic institutions.

There have been significant consequences. In a voluntary community lacking the powers of taxation the task of financing so many philanthropic needs has created a psychology and climate of its own. Fund raising is no longer what it once was, a subordinate appendage to Jewish communal life. In many ways it now dominates the community and is of the essence in the volunteer layman's participation in what is needed to get the community's work done. This is increasingly true, even for organizations not directly involved in fund raising but whose purpose is community service.

On the basis of membership the largest of these are Hadassah and B'nai B'rith. Hadassah supports a magnificent medical and social service program in Israel; B'nai B'rith sponsors a multiplicity of Jewish services in education, civic defense, youth guidance, aid to Israel and social welfare. While both organizations maintain direct member-participation activities (B'nai B'rith, for example, does so in its programs of citizenship and civic affairs, adult Jewish education, services to the armed forces and veterans) the organic relationship between the Hadassah member or B'nai

B'rith member and the organization's professionally-administered service programs is in many cases reduced to a single fact—the raising of funds.

This, in its own way, exacts the inherent price—even penalty—of bigness and specialization. It is decried, with some justification, as impeding widespread and diverse community participation in Jewish affairs or as providing an unsatisfying expression for such participation. Not everyone finds fund raising a fully adequate outlet for volunteer work.

Still, fund raising is not a confined process. In its modern metamorphosis it has become a program, with weighty propagative effect among the volunteers and subscribers drawn into its orbit. Thus, fund raising is creatively functional in its own way, providing values above and beyond that of attracting money. It helps rivet public attention on the institution supported; it inspires a sense of mutuality between the institution and its supporters.

These are plus factors which would seem to argue in favor of a greater number of "independent" campaigns rather than of one federated appeal, the procedure which is prevalent in organized Jewish life. If the community's manpower could be properly mobilized to conduct separate drives for every deserving institution we would, in the nature of things, have a livelier Jewish community. But such mobilization cannot be fairly allocated or automated and there is not enough good available voluntary manpower. Many institutions, of importance to Jewish life but with understandable difficulties in evoking strong organizational loyalties, would suffer even more than they do now from the zeal of the disciplined constituencies of other organizations. In a fully competitive market of multiple drives, the spoils would go disproportionately to the more powerful and vocal groups, without relation to actual needs and values.

This could well entrap the general contributor, bewilder him with confusion, harass him by noisy competition and leave him in perpetual uncertainty as to how he can express his altruism effectively and wisely.

To avoid the pitfalls, American Jewry drew in part on the experiences of the *kehilla* of the Old World and created the local community fund. This *federation* movement, established in Boston in 1895 to support a number of local health and social service agencies, progressed slowly until the 1920's, when the *welfare fund,* centralizing fund raising for national Jewish agencies, came into being. By that time many local Jewish programs of a "nonsectarian" nature—hospitals, orphanages, care of the aged—had been incorporated in general "community chests" which had made their appearance during World War I.

The distinction between federation and welfare fund has disappeared through the unification of these bodies over the years. They now exist as separate entities in only a few of the more than two hundred communities which support united funds.

The greatest momentum for the growth of the welfare funds came with the advent of the United Jewish Appeal and expanded even more rapidly in the frantic spurt of activity immediately following World War II.

By and large, federated fund raising has proven to be the best method yet devised to give some rational coherence to Jewish philanthropy. It is designed to—and generally does—reduce the administrative cost of raising money. For all of its monopoly it cannot raise as much money—perhaps surprisingly—as can pressures and appeals, in their total, of strong independent campaigns that are supposedly in competition with one another.

In the mathematics of modern fund raising the sum of the parts can be greater than the whole. For a human equation comes into play: a contributor who cannot bring himself to give less than twenty-five dollars each to five separate institutions finds his conscience and his status unaffected as a contributor of one hundred dollars to the five when they are united in a single campaign.

This is not a universal rule of the contributor's behavior. In the formative days of federations another factor emerged. At that time the collective effort was to provide for local agencies, themselves unable to dramatize their needs and financial requirements. Federation came to their rescue by its embracing mass appeal and a hundred-dollar giver often represented "new money" —a fresh source previously completely untapped.

Like all simplifying theories, this is now valid only up to a point—the point where the individual though federated institution is as competent and knowledgeable in raising funds as is the federation itself, and where there is a rationale at hand for the contributor to give in the aggregate less to a one-time appeal.

There has also been a change in the direction of Jewish philanthropy—at least in that part of it retained for domestic purposes. It is no longer, as it once was, a Lady Bountiful act of "the rich helping the poor." Problems of poverty, health, and old age are now being met, in some measure, by the general social welfare government agencies. Jewish fund raising today is largely for the Jewish community's self-services—for Israel, for civic defense, for its religious education, for its youth guidance, and for other clearly purposed Jewish *group* activities. "Giver" and "beneficiary" are one and the same. But while charity for the individual was its own justification, philanthropy for the community now also has ideological overtones that can attract (or repel) the loyalties of the contributor.

When these factors are considered, there are national organizations and institutions, skilled at fund raising and ideologically attractive, that find the organized federation not necessarily a boon. They accept federation allotments knowing that, by doing so, they sacrifice their own special potentials. This, "for the sake of the community."

This is a drawback that is supposed to be overcome—if not always compensated for—by the projected image of a central fund as qualified to allocate the community's dollars with some measure of equity. It is patent that five separate institutions in a community are not necessarily of equal priority, nor are their budgetary needs the same. The contributor, in his innocence or with his status code, is incapable himself of allowing for the differences and imbalances. This is palpably true in the case of our friend who gives an equal twenty-five dollars to five causes. His action may also involve a neglect of the needs of other institutions in the community whose history and appeals have somehow not registered with him, or emerged too late for his rational review.

His gift to a united fund—even when reduced in total—has the virtue of correcting inequities that would otherwise be perpetuated by force of habit and inertia.

It is at this point that the united fund serves its primary purposes. It clears away the jungle of confusion; it achieves some degree of orderliness and equity; and it plays a unifying role in Jewish life.

The united fund has therefore become a useful and necessary structure, of pragmatic value, at least until something equally unifying and still more equitable comes along. It has established for itself a growing—and sometimes cumbersomely large—influence in Jewish affairs and the community in turn has acquired a vested interest in the continuity of its federations and welfare funds.

The question is: How can we improve them?

## 2.

One conspicuous element in the united fund development is the tendency to give undue emphasis to the fund raising process itself. By a kind of Parkinson's law, the federated fund acquires a life, quality and aggressive vitality of its own—and these are not always organically subordinated to the ends for which the funds have been established.

Essentially, two parties are involved in fund raising: the contributor and the beneficiary. The united fund obscures this relationship when it becomes a third principal with so dominant and demanding a character of its own as to subordinate and put into the shade the parties that have created the fund as a convenient machine. The machine comes to master its creator.

Now, this criticism does not suggest that a united fund can exist or serve its purposes as a nonentity. The image of the united fund must be clear if it is to have status, enlist mass support, and provide the trappings and prestige always needed to develop a leadership capable of exerting its proper influence.

But a line of demarcation between the fund and its partners, however hazy and indistinct, does—and should—exist. When the fund oversteps it to become, at least in its own eyes, more vital

than the member agencies it is organized to serve, there is a
jarring inversion of values; the machinery has taken on an importance beyond that of its purpose. A common distressing experience
among agencies enrolled in a united fund is that their identity for
contributors becomes blurred and public understanding of why
they exist and what they are trying to do is, by a magician's
sleight of hand, diverted to the fund and its own overpowering
reality.

It would be revealing to test the knowledge individual contributors have of the institutions and agencies that share in their
common fund. My own informal observations are that it is the rare
person indeed who is able to so much as identify the thirty to fifty
organizations united in some of the larger funds, much less know
their purposes, programs, and values. Probably not more than one
person in ten has a name acquaintanceship with, at best, one-third
of the agencies that share in the general subsidy that he helps provide. At a United Jewish Appeal gathering in New York I tested
my curiosity on this point by informally polling about two dozen
persons who were present—each a contributor of one thousand
dollars or more. As I recall, only about half scored correctly on
naming the six affiliates of the New York UJA campaign.*

As an offset to this obscuring of organizational individuality,
small institutions, it is said, are better off in a united fund; they
are able to ride on the coattails of skillfully advertised or in-
trinsically "emotional giving" for Israel that nowadays is the
prized salespiece of packaged Jewish fund raising.

I do not know how valid this contention is. There are un-
doubtedly marginal groups in a fund; and there is the recurring
question as to whether they rightfully belong there at all. Others,
vital to Jewish survival—Jewish education is an example—are
generally not so organically constituted as to be able to finance
themselves; they need the shelter of a fund. But for a third

---

* These are the United Israel Appeal (I dare not test anyone on *its* constituent agencies!), the Joint Distribution Committee, the National Jewish
Welfare Board, the American Jewish Congress, the United HIAS Service,
and the New York Association for New Americans.

category of programs, popular in their appeal, and sustained by a vital rank and file support, central fund raising can mean reduced income along with a diminished public awareness. These are perhaps unavoidable imbalances. Kept within moderate bounds they are to be accepted as, on the whole, a modest price for a measure of unity and harmony in Jewish affairs.

A more unfortunate development is that of the fund that reaches out vertically to tower over all institutions and to establish itself in its own right as the dominant force in Jewish life. This is in contrast to the normal, wide-embracing, organic, and what might be called horizontal coalition of beneficiary institutions, rooted in a public's loyalty to their services and programs.

The vertical threat is perhaps more a frame of mind than a calculated program of conquest. Whatever its motivation, it introduces what I regard as a monolithic imposition of decisions from the top down. Thereby it inverts the solid structure of the pyramid of public generosity and of its allocations by standing the pyramid on its head—and the instability quickly becomes apparent.

Whenever a united fund leadership abandons the character of serving as a pragmatic instrument for the existing institutions and it sets out to become their master, the character of the beneficiary agency, based upon its many years of experience, is at once threatened. If the agency submits, it finds itself thrust into a Procrustean bed. It loses its distinction and the unique values of its experiences and history. Instead of planning its program, procedure, and budget with single-minded attention to its purposes and the needs of the time, it must begin to compromise its convictions, to close its eyes on its own judgments, in order to appease the "vertical"-minded united fund patrons.

And so the acceptance of the authority of a vertically reaching united fund ends up by crippling agency independence. At the same time, it narrows the base of community life by its de-emphasis of the community's *functional* activities. When the fund inhibits the Jewish public from sharing directly and freely in the institutions, there is a corresponding loss of interest in them. The intrusive fund weakens the loyalties between the people and the institutions they have created or worked with, and thereby destroys the indispensable element in public service—the human element.*

No American Jew is obligated to belong to any organization. When he chooses to participate personally in some phase of Jewish life his efforts must be welcomed as *identification* with the interests of the community—the cardinal step toward Jewish continuity. A fund vertically rigid and so dominant frustrates the very unity in whose name it speaks.

### 3.

Big givers predominate in the fund's councils. Their persuasive influence, for good or ill, largely determines policy.† The con-

* The experience of the Joint Defense Appeal, a horizontal-type fund-raising agency acting nationally on behalf of the American Jewish Committee and the Anti-Defamation League of B'nai B'rith, offers an instructive case history. In 1947 this fund-raising agency, a constituent of most local welfare funds, agreed to extend this policy to New York and Chicago, the only major American cities without over-all federated fund raising. In New York, JDA became a constituent of the United Jewish Appeal; in Chicago it joined with that city's Combined Jewish Appeal (which combines only a fraction of Chicago's Jewish institutions). The decision to foresake independent campaigns in the two principal centers of Jewish population was made by JDA's leadership as a concession to unity, and only after long debate on the wisdom of dimming JDA's identity by such a move.

The arrangement lasted four years. It was amicably severed when curtailed receipts in both cities drastically reduced JDA's income. It took several years for JDA to scrape the rust from its apparatus and to energize the volunteer leadership and campaign teams that had been in limbo during the years of affiliation with UJA. Its reactivated leadership, to raise funds successfully, had to know *why* and *what for* to make its case to contributors. This meant keeping a constant and lively interest in civic defense problems as well as in the activities of the two JDA agencies. In the natural process, this interest led to increased activity and greater loyalty. JDA soon restored itself to satisfactory levels of income.

Since the JDA agencies work in the highly-exposed areas of anti-Semitism and civic defense, their problem of maintaining individualism and identity is far less acute than that of most organizations hidden in a welfare fund. But it is also JDA's wise policy to speak *for* these organizations rather than in terms of itself.

† This, in part, is also a hangover from the early composition of federations. These were organized, financed and directed by German-oriented Jews, the patricians of what was then an ethnic-separated American Jewry. The latecoming Eastern Europeans were largely on the *receiving* end of the first federated charities.

tention that the leadership of a fund is "representative of the community" may be only a "paper fact." Often this is rationalized as a "realistic" necessity. Democratizing a fund's directorate, admittedly good in principle, is supposed to be bad for the balance sheet, if the interest of wealthier contributors is diminished by limiting their authority and status. There is also the position that it is not entirely undemocratic to allot to the big contributor a correspondingly big voice. Whatever the theory, the practice very often effectively forecloses the opportunity for leadership and policy-making by those who, out of personal circumstances, cannot meet the standard of "big giving" but who have much to contribute in thinking, in policy appraisals, and in other forms of active participation.

Controlled by local personalities, the fund is first of all responsive to local needs for which no one else will provide. Home town pressures give local institutions a priority that is reflected in the fund's allocations. Partisan pressures from a big giver do as much for "pet" institutions located outside the community itself. There is the case of a welfare fund in a Southeastern metropolis that makes an annual subvention to a small Yeshiva in New York. This is not an allocation to assist the many Yeshivot in New York that help preserve traditional Judaism—but to one in particular and only that one. Its leader, a dynamic *rebbe,* had visited the community and strongly influenced one of its big givers who has a powerful voice in the local fund. Since then, year in and out, the same Yeshiva has been favored.

On the opposite end of the local and parochial influences are the overseas programs. These have a drama and "crisis" appeal around which the fund organizes its campaign. They too tend to acquire a high priority status. And they have the strength to enforce this position if it is ever threatened.

Other national institutions concerned with the advancement of Jewish life in America are caught in a grinding middle. They are not "crisis"-ridden and cannot cry out for support in terms of rescue and rehabilitation of Jews. They are not adequately spoken for in local communities. They generally do not—even if they should—command priority status.

This disadvantage is further aggravated by a united fund's concern for an exclusive monopolistic status in the community. To avoid separate, competing independent campaigns, the fund —often unconsciously—resorts to "buying off" tactics, accepting into the ranks of its beneficiaries an institution or agency it might otherwise reject, paying unconscionably for its "nuisance value."

This is a polite and widely accepted form of community blackmail. Allocations to "nuisance" groups, multiplied over the years, account for a considerable amount of money. The practice is just neither to the contributor nor to the legitimate agencies. It reveals a major weakness—a willingness to compromise for the appearance, if not the reality, of unity.

Meanwhile, one united fund after another, heavily committed to the skyrocketing needs of our overseas programs, has failed to meet the minimum needs of its domestic national affiliates.

And at this point a familiar phenomenon appears. What happens when the head of the family can't pay the bills? The wife finds a supplementary job. This has become the pattern in Jewish fund raising. The domestic national affiliate has to be given its head and allowed to meet the deficit with its own *supplemental* campaigns.

The fund is not happy about this. There are irritating questions: Where will all this stop? If a supplemental campaign is permissible for one national institution, why not for another? And how long before orderly fund raising is reduced to a shambles?

These questions arise out of a mistaken image of what a fund is meant to be. The fund is a rational approach, achieving efficiency at some slight sacrifice of sentiment and loyalties. But it is not in and of itself meant to be a monolithic instrument, ordained to raise *all* the philanthropic money available in the community. For, as in every economic development, there comes a point of diminishing returns.

New York City is a lively example. Its sprawling Jewish community cannot be brought completely into a single central fund. Along with its near-chaos of an uncounted number of independent appeals, it has a few elements of coordination—the UJA, the Federation of Jewish Philanthropies, the JDA. These are worthwhile experiences for centralizing several appeals. But while important, they are not pre-emptive: arbitrarily to consolidate all the institutional needs into one massive structure would stultify Jewish life in the world's largest community of Jews.

Of the sixty-five to eighty million dollars (after collection "shrinkage," administration and other costs) raised outside New York City by the federations and welfare funds each year, more than 65 per cent is allocated for overseas purposes. More than one-fourth of the total is retained for local agencies. Substantially less than 10 per cent is distributed for the support of national institutions. This last group, however, requires nearly fifty million dollars a year (or about one-half of what American Jewry sends overseas) for its cultural, religious, educational, community welfare, and civic defense programs on the national scale on which the agencies operate. This means that every dollar allocated for these purposes by united funds must be matched by nine or ten dollars raised somehow, somewhere by the institutions themselves. That they have, in fact, succeeded in this formidable task demonstrates that the united fund as a universal structure embracing all loyalties still falls far short of the communities' capacity for philanthropy.

This being so, independent and supplemental campaigns, in a proper context, are not the evils or temporary stopgaps that the more ardent proponents of central funds believe them to be. There is still a place in the structure of the community for major fund-raising efforts that fly in the face of theoretical blueprints. For there is still an imbalance in the united fund structure.

True, it sets out to represent the contributing public to income-seeking institutions and, conversely, to represent these institutions to its contributors. Most united funds, however, dramatize themselves persuasively as protectors of the contributor and, in the process, bypass their corresponding role as the fund-raising spokesman *for* the beneficiary agencies. Not because the fund must make a choice between them as conflicting interests. In the nature of things, contributor and beneficiary are not competitive, but complementary; they pursue the same goals. Frequently the outlook of the fund is rather an expression of its tendency, above all, for a dominance in the community.

I am mindful of the fund in one community that probed the budgets of its member-agencies with the attitude of an inquisitor. An agency's budget was not just studied; its representatives were brutally grilled. This went on for several months each year. Yet each year the united fund's income declined. This the fund's director found hard to understand.

But the experience is not really baffling. The constant assaults on the capacity of the agencies to decide what needed doing undermined the community's confidence. Energies and enthusiasms were diverted from raising contributions to policing agencies' budgets. A united fund that spends the largest part of its energies in inquisitional challenge of the agencies it supports has little time and less spirit for fund raising itself. Like a simpleton farmer, it uproots each plant to see how it is coming along.

A more rational approach might be to balance a fund's leadership with representation from both sides. Specifically, the national agencies affiliated with most welfare funds might be invited to appoint their representatives, preferably from within the community, to the fund's directorate.

Nothing of this sort happens. The fund's leadership normally represents what is in reality only half of the intended partnership —the contributors. If a spokesman for an affiliated institution is appointed to a fund's leadership, this is incidental to and eclipsed by his role as a contributor. Yet such happenstance can be decisive in a fund's allocations. The fortunate institution finds itself with some supporters, the luckless one is left voiceless and undefended. In the next community, this may work the other way around. The arrangement can hardly pass as "orderly."

The changing character of the Jewish community is subtle and continuing. But change as an element of progress also needs to be recognized and encouraged. The united fund, however, has shown itself sluggish toward adjustments in Jewish life.

The signs of change have long been visible—and it was a

responsibility of community leadership to take due note that the expanding postwar birth rate and the heightened interest in religion would quickly exceed available resources for youth guidance and Jewish education. If the central funds have recognized these forces at all, they have done so only recently. Except when roused by critical urgency—as in the case of Israel's needs—the fund lags behind the times. Its tempo is determined by the *status quo ante*. Its criteria are its own past performances. The question "How much did we give X agency last year?" becomes the cardinal factor in fund allocations.

4.

The sharpest criticism of the united fund can be directed at its efforts, peremptory if well-intentioned, to *control* the community. Moved by an addiction to a comptroller's tidiness, and strong in its grip on the public's purse, many a fund has misinterpreted its role as that of the benevolent, all-knowing rich uncle of Jewish life.

The original purpose of the central fund—to reduce waste and duplication by *collecting* the community's institutions in a common fund-raising apparatus—is clear and unchallenged. To split the kitty with some regard for equity the fund also engages in a *coordinating* process, reviewing institution budgets as a guide to its allocations.

Here the confusion starts. The competency of the united fund to examine and judge budgets, in view of the deficiencies of its own limited leadership, is a contestable issue. All the more so in light of the fact that the procedures of budget reviewing and the standards used vary from fund to fund.*

* The Large Cities Budgeting Conference (now embracing nineteen of the larger united funds) was established to engage cooperatively in budget studies as a guide toward improved allocation standards. The method is fine; the limitation is that LCBC is not a uniquely qualified or disinterested body. Its policy makers are precisely the same leaders as that of the funds that comprise it. Thus, virtues and faults are unchanged, and the persistent shortcomings of partisanship, local pressures, personal philosophies, and inadequate understanding of the total community that afflict the budget reviewing

Is it at all the prerogative of a fund to evaluate budgets?

There is, to be sure, a strong view critical of any action by a fund beyond its use as a collection service. Contradicting this, however, is the fund's responsibility to the contributor—that his generosity be put to the most productive use. To do this, the fund must, of necessity, exercise some degree of judgment. It cannot be hemmed in by a formula in which every slice of the pie is precut, the only issue being the size of the pie.

So the fund determines that it must think for itself. It must "evaluate." But evaluate what? At this juncture lies the conflict between the fund's legitimate aspiration to try to *coordinate* and its sometimes subconscious efforts to reach out for *control*.

What does coordinate mean? It means that a fund can properly disallow expansion of a local child care program (that is, it can limit its allocation) when in its judgment an increase in cultural activities is more important to the community's welfare. Similarly, it can decide that occupational guidance should have more of the money it has collected than, say, a program of historical research. It can scrupulously investigate the extent of the service a national agency provides its particular community as one of its yardsticks for its allocations to that agency. In short, the propriety (if not always the ability) of the fund *in considering the costs of community institutions, one against the other, as they relate to Jewish life, local, national, or world-wide,* is generally accepted. This is the *coordinating* function of the fund.

At the same time, this role has its own natural but definite limitations. These are transgressed when the fund begins to probe the community's institutions *qualitatively*. This is where the threat begins of *controlling* the wider community. The fund that is qualified to determine its allocation for local child care by judging this activity in relation to other local community needs, is *not* qualified to say *how* a child-care program should operate and which techniques it should use or discard. These are functional decisions.

---

of most funds are not necessarily absent when LCBC pursues this task, although it must be said that some of LCBC's leadership strives mightily to overcome these difficulties.

The authority to make them must remain with the operative institution itself.

To illustrate further: the fund cannot determine a hospital's administration despite (or precisely because of) its role of fund-raiser for that hospital. It cannot judge pedagogic studies prepared by the American Association for Jewish Education, or the curriculum of a seminary, notwithstanding its allocation to both groups. It is not qualified nor must it take upon itself the prerogative to say whether a brief *amicus* filed by the American Jewish Congress is good community relations or bad for the entire country. It cannot decide on the workings of B'nai B'rith Hillel student programs. When it seeks to reach out into these areas as part of its allocation process the fund is veering toward control of the community by asserting a super-authoritarianism over the community's institutions. And the practice is foredoomed. What we have learned from the past abortive efforts for enforced Jewish unity has its values for those federations and welfare funds that tend to overreach themselves.*

There is a delightful story attributed to Rabbi Herbert Friedman, the forceful executive vice-chairman of UJA, that bears repeating.

A national UJA leader, touring the country to quicken enthusiasm for still another year's campaign, addressed a group of volunteer workers. Many of them, old hands at UJA drives, had heard the speaker's theme—"crisis" . . . "emergency"—for sev-

---

* Does this mean that an institution seeking public funds is sacrosanct? Hardly. The right to judge its worth rests with the community itself—in this case, the contributor. The distinction between fund and contributor is that the latter, not the fund, is the superior authority. It is authority, however, which the contributor cannot delegate to the fund since the fund, also representing the affiliated institutions, is not free to accept it.

How then can the contributor assert his judgment? When he contributes through a united fund—he can't; no more than he can be selective in his support of any federated institution. This is a penalty of central fund raising. On the other side, the institution, by submitting to coordinated allocations, likewise surrenders a measure of its own independence and freedom to finance itself.

eral years running. Repetition did not leave them indifferent to the high stakes, the human lives, involved. It did, however, raise a small question in one volunteer's mind that, on the first opportunity, he put to the speaker.

"Friend," he began, "what you said here is all too true—the desperate need to save Jews . . . a new life for them in Israel . . . jobs and homes . . . security . . . rescue dollars . . . run to the banks to borrow millions, run a campaign to collect the millions . . . repeat it all next year—I understand all that.

"But—just one question. These constant crises . . . one hundred million dollar campaigns—when will it all end? Give us an inkling, something to look forward to, can you?"

The UJA official thought for a moment. "Sure," he said.

"Well—when?"

"In the year of the Messiah," the UJA man said. "Plus one."

The volunteer sadly nodded his head in understanding. Except —"Why the extra year?"

The UJA man explained. "One final campaign—to pay off the banks!"

The story has its built-in moral. American Jewry shuddered in disbelief when the first one hundred million dollar emergency campaign was projected. Yet on that day organized Jewish philanthropy faced a new horizon. The "emergency" is now also the commonplace. There is little indication, over the long, inflationary haul, that the Jewish community will ever revert to the pre-Israel level of fund raising. In a growing community new demands are sure to spring up to replace the old.

With this prospect, the federated fund is entrusted with an increasingly greater importance in Jewish life. Criticism of some developments cannot shut out the explicit virtues; and surely the united fund is and can be a pliable instrument for *voluntary* unity, with the community infinitely better off because of it.

*If*—it does not overreach itself.

I have pointed to some dangers. But I know that the problems of Jewish philanthropy are not going to be settled by jurisprudence or by an official rulebook. For one thing, the rules get fouled up in the net of their own contradictions. And, for another, the course of Jewish life in America will continue to be guided by its voluntary spirit.

How, then, to measure and foresee the fund's role in the community? Isaiah had a suggestion, as wise as it is simple. "Come now," he said, "and let us reason together."

The rule of reason!

It is not self-operative. To apply the rule of reason to Jewish fund raising presupposes a mutuality, a sense of confidence, and a wise regard for all the parties.

The successful fund—meaning the fund that reaches a high level of income—finds itself, quite naturally and without unpleasantness, in the best position to influence its member-agencies in the mutual reasoning process so essential to agency and fund alike. This should strengthen the fund—which needs strengthening if it is to meet the new tasks ahead.

The fund must carry out its role with respect for moderation. It must control its urge to control. It must broaden its leadership. It must come to understand and make adjustments for the changing character of Jewish life. Above all, the fund must be guided in what it does by the most important thing it is supposed to do: **Not to manage the community's money. To raise it.**

# (6)

## *Who Sits on the Dais?*

Interpreters of Jewish life in America, whatever else they disagree on, close ranks on the subject of Jewish leadership. They find it wanting. There may be clashing convictions over the qualities needed by a community leader. There is common agreement—often expressed with a melancholy sigh and head-shaking—that whoever the genuine leaders are, there are not enough of them.

More sardonic observers will suggest that the shortage is in direct proportion to the surplus of banquet *balabatim,* a breed readily identifiable at Jewish affairs and inevitably congregated conspicuously at the head table. The protocol that places them there generally reflects a community's struggle (and compromise) with its leadership requirements.

I am not one to decry *noblesse oblige*. After all, I generally can find my own place card up front on the speakers' table. Nor do I need an exponent of the "let's-be-practical" school to remind me that more work is done for a useful cause, and more money flows into its support, through *yichus* (pride of status) than through the more recondite urges of compassion. I am in favor of being practical; add another row to the dais if that will help! (The record, in my experience, is eight tiers—a fund-raising dinner at which the toastmaster relieved my initial misgivings when he assured me that we did not outnumber the audience.) But it is also a practical matter that Jewish leadership must be something more than a well-groomed display over the dinner platters of roast beef, which increasingly, in today's Jewish community, is kosher.

There is nothing new under the sun or under the ballroom lights. Each generation has wailed over the absence of adequate leadership since it is only in retrospect and with some historical perspective that a leadership can be properly evaluated.

It may be that we are being served better than we think. Yet a critical look has the virtue of trying to make things better than they are.

A constant, scratching treasure hunt for Jewish leaders has become a community parlor game. Precisely what is being searched for is not always clearly defined. Who can really inventory the qualities necessary for Jewish leadership at different times and under varying circumstances? Enough that Jewish life is fertile with an endless variety of institutional forms—a synagogue on one corner and a temple opposite; a burial society here and a council there to rehabilitate Jewish convicts; an organization to teach Hebrew and another to preserve Yiddish. These must all be properly outfitted with presidents and chairmen and officers of the board, executive directors and group workers, rabbis and fund-raisers. Real leaders among laymen or professional career men are, if we insist on excellence, in short supply.

Voluntary Jewish leadership—that is, the policy-making lay leaders—if it is to give meaningful direction to Jewish needs and aspirations, is inherently a sobering experience. It must cope with the uncertain behavior of a Jewish community that is still some-what young in its Jewish expressions; impulsive; without fully es-tablished internal communications; contradictory by nature and incapable, in a voluntary society, of policing itself. Many a com-munity resembles an unreined team free to gallop every which way. Or else it is stubborn, impossible to budge from its com-placency. These are frustrations for any leadership. A timid lead-ership will take comfort in conformity and in a policy of drift leading to ineptness. The man who was running at the tail end of a mob explained his actions by pointing out that "he had to—he was their leader." But unless it prods the community into motion and persuades it into purposeful directions, it isn't leadership at all. It is dais décor.

Harry Truman, discussing leadership in politics, put it colorfully when he said: "If you can't stand the heat, get out of the kitchen." This must be stressed in Jewish life as well. A vast leadership potential in the community is never realized among personalities with talents and first-rate minds because they are unwilling—more exactly, uninspired or uninvited—to stand the heat of the kitchen. By contrast, we have occupants of leadership comfortable and smug in their status quo chairs of authority—they never go near the kitchen. We also have those who grasp for, or are pushed into, leadership and who, lacking an intimate insight into Jewish hopes and problems, can't even find the kitchen.

A struggling, badly outnumbered minority has the knowledge or willingness to learn, the patience and personality traits for crea-tive leadership, and a talent for the best of community service. It is as yet much too small in number and the constant problem is how to increase its ranks.

There are less inspiring aspects of Jewish leadership: a Jewish cultural innocence, an unawareness of Jewish history and tradi-tion—the marks most often of the community's "secular-loaded," "Torah-abandoned," "checkbook" Judaism. "A community gets the kind of leadership it deserves," the saying goes. This is a surface explanation, and, within its limits, not inaccurate. To an extent, leadership must always reflect the colorations and cross currents of the community from which it springs.

For better or worse, but certainly as a mirror of contemporary times, the businessman-philanthropist has increasingly replaced the rabbi-scholar as the influential personality in Jewish leadership. Yet, the good intentions of the Jewish community are thwarted by the helter-skelter way it selects its leaders.

In our research-minded age few enterprises fail to analyze their problems in terms of the people they need to meet definable responsibilities. The Jewish community, a heavily capitalized enterprise, does not. It makes do, by and large, with catch-as-catch-can selections. Whether the community is not yet sophisticated enough to pinpoint its real leadership needs or is drugged by an overpowering inertia, the effect is the same and is depressingly visible in one area after another. Positions of leadership go begging . . . and the woefully unqualified, impelled by ego drives, go begging for them and often win by default. When this happens the community becomes in effect—although not to outward appearance—leaderless.

The random approach—I have seen a decisive choice made on the toss of a coin—is sometimes forced on the community; at other times it grows out of the stagnant conditions. In either case, there is little order and less understanding of the character of leadership needed to advance Jewish life in America.

I know that fault-finding is easy; in fact, there is one syndrome of discussion on the shortcomings of Jewish leadership that comes ready-made, prepackaged and primed for violent delivery. It includes (1) a pat indictment of the process by which a man's wealth and secular status rather than his Jewish knowledge and insights have become the qualifications for a Jewish aristocracy, and (2) a defiant reminder that we are doomed to sterility in Jewish terms until rabbis and scholars are restored, as of old, as a pre-eminent leadership force in the community.

But merely to raise this outcry is not enough, the more so when much of the argument ignores the realities of current Jewish life. It presupposes an imaginary rather than the real Jewish community or one that can conceivably emerge from our emancipated environment. Leadership in such a free community cannot be artificially created by a preplotted course (however necessary it is that we plan). It is bound to hinge on and develop out of external events—that are always changing in substance or at least in emphasis. If we have elevated the "money man" into the highest posts of leadership, the unparallelled compulsions of a philanthropy-centered community had something to do with the selection.

In an earlier chapter I ventured the heretical opinion that the rabbi, with his unique capacity as religious specialist, is not thereby automatically qualified for community leadership in areas outside the pulpit or the religious school. His scholarship and training give him an equipment not as readily had by the Jewish businessman. But it is not, of itself, a resource for general leadership, certainly not in fields remote from his training. Nothing in his clerical history entitles him to be the central force in the wide-ranging Jewish life that goes on outside the synagogue. There are rabbis and scholars who prefer to live their lives outside, or some distance removed from, the moving streams of important daily events that are significant for the community, and that in no way stem from the life of prayer and meditation. We assume as an article of faith that rabbis are as intimately informed on Jewish current events as we expect them to be with on Jewish life of past civilizations. Curious, but the fact is that it isn't so. Few American Jews are, whether in positions of leadership or not.

In present-day Jewish life we eagerly reach out for the substance of leadership. The instinctive response of the community to such personalities as Stephen Wise and Abba Hillel Silver, both products of the rabbinate, to Dr. Abram Sachar, a scholar, and to Henry Monsky, a lawyer who acquired his Jewish insights out of a secular background, suggests that we prefer to follow the man in active motion. In each of these modern giants of Jewish leadership there was a spark of urgency; each was an imaginative architect of nonconformist designs; each was ready to experiment, to chart new roads. Their common quality was not religious excellence, or classic scholarship, or, for that matter, a lack of these. What marked them with a radiant glow, visible to all, was their subtle attunement to what Jewish life asked for and needed at a given time, and their willingness to do something about it. They were activists. Rabbi or scholar or lawyer, they made their impact alike, and in what strict constructionists would categorize as the "secular aspects of Judaism."

Even if the first call of community leadership were reserved for scholars and for leaders from our clergy—those who in the tradition of Ezra and Hillel were alertly alive to contemporary Jewish affairs and were creatively able "to do something about it"—the wider problem of marshaling and expanding Jewish leadership would still not be met or even significantly reduced. For the current motivations in Jewish life lead to a small ratio of Jewish scholars as against, let us say, lawyers, or business administrators, or real estate operators, many of them with a vibrant conscience and a curiosity that carry them into the tide of Jewish events.

In searching for able and active leadership we may as well accept the fact that the image of the businessman-leader on the dais is here to stay—and explore ways to improve his Jewishness.

## 2.

In a qualification test for everyone who aspired to leadership in Jewish life, I would include three questions as fundamental. There are others I can think of but I am ready to accept the right answers to these:

Is he patient with the community, its institutions, its differences, even its weaknesses, but impatient with its pessimists?

Does he think Jewishly?

Will he, when the time comes, move over and make room for another aspirant to leadership?

Moses' parting message to Israel was "Thou shalt choose life," meaning not life as a mere passive existence but as the fullest expression of the vital potentials of the era in which we measure our days.

Jewish leadership must come from those who have leaped up to "choose life." It must challenge the status quo while giving tradition its due respect. It must be sensitive to movement and change, as well as to the history that made us what we are. It must reject the encrusted and the outmoded tradition—the ways of mere habit that try, unbecomingly, to don the robes of tradition.

In my lifetime, Jewish leadership has had to grapple with cataclysmic change. There was the advent of Nazism and the embittering discovery that few Jewish leaders here or abroad fully grasped the enormity of the disaster that it projected. We may not have stayed Hitler's madness—a world coalition was needed to strike it down—but we might have marshalled greater resources and done much, much more in terms of human rescue.

On a happier note, when Ben-Gurion, flanked by the ministers of a provisional government, announced the establishment of Israeli statehood, the whole texture of Jewish life in America was affected by a revolutionary change; and we were not much more prepared, although we did rush to make up—and make amends —for lost time. The ways of yesterday no longer applied; they were out of date or had to be magnified to such proportions as to constitute a new frontier. Jewish leaders who had dragged their heels for or against the concept of a restored Jewish national homeland were forced to abandon their shuffling pace or, once and for all, forfeit their claims to leadership.

Whatever one's philosophical outlook on the emergence of Israel as a state with a Jewish majority, to have ignored its impact on the American Jewish community could only mean a mulish acceptance of blindfolds as an improvement in vision—a total rejection of reality. When spokesmen for organized anti-Zionism, dismayed at the massive transformation in sentiment that had taken place, tried to exorcise the apparition by wishful fantasies they fell out of step with history. Certainly there is room in Jewish life for a legitimate anti-Zionist leadership. But what pretends to that role today seems to me an incantation in monotone, mesmerized, meaningless where it is not damaging.

The Hitler era and the rebirth of Israel, extremes in Jewish experience, are vivid illustrations that Jewish life does not stand still. Less dramatic developments in day-to-day Jewish existence tell the same story. It is both a task and a test of Jewish leadership to be alertly sensitive to these changes.

There is, too, a voluble element in Jewish leadership that is intellectually alive to what is going on and that yet denies its demonstrated vitality. Afflicted with a sense of doom, it exhausts itself in gloomy assessments that Jewish life is disintegrating and that its demise is foreseeable.

This is not an innovation of our times. It is part of an ageless echo of imminent doom. The persistence of our people has been matched, in unbroken tradition, by the persistence of those forever scanning the horoscope and forecasting an end to Jewish continuity. From the angry prophets of Biblical Judaism to the pessimists of our own generation, Jewish life has had its Cassandras who saw only the collapse and not the reconstruction; the disaster, not the rebirth.

These despairing minds, genuinely concerned with the future of Judaism, cast accusing glances at the new temples in suburbia, at the fund-raising banquets, at the sisterhoods' theater parties— at the many material evidences of a secular-framed Judaism— and dismiss it as lacking any spiritual meaning and as unsuitable for Jewish survival.

They may be right. But their impatience is unjustified and their rancor misdirected. They scold the community—the people and their institutions. Their energies might better be focused on an evolving Jewish life that has the capacity for sturdy growth. Only a leadership inspired by optimism, and as patient with people as it must be dissatisfied with the status quo, will do this.

A leadership that sees only disaster on the horizon will act by its depressed vision and rationalize what it does in gloomy terms. Such a leadership we can do without. If we believe there is a happy destiny for Jewish life in America we ought to choose a leadership that believes it too.

How we can evoke a Jewish leadership that will be conscious of and responsive to Jewish values is itself a problem. The leadership of every generation is colored by its own life experiences. Mine, tragically, went through an unchartered transition from the immigrant culture of its fathers to something new and still inchoate, having first largely depleted itself of Jewish knowledge and intuition. The pendulum is now moving the other way in search of

this is not the

the impulse
ther than out

re I challenge
hropy. There
. The crucial
hip.
ot a boast. I
e, *shechita*—
ing for many
hotly-debated
brought more
On then pend-
ps, a distinct
s mine; to en-
wish thing to

of no conse-
le segment of
matter of tra-
point of view
ness, however
nity.
ent of Jewish
sion. It must
vitable, more
st the back-
particular or-
or moderated
ship to relate

ssure. It does
Its leadership
many of its

One encrusted form of
lodged: self-perpetuating
the highest levels of Jewis
   It is hard to tell just
quired its strength. No d
awe and subconscious ca
before those whom they
an advocate's skill in the
tained by the ego-indulg
render or even to share th
   I recall a meeting ma
Astoria attended by four
Each was head of an imp
was perpetually in office
proprietors rather than e
say it was a token of their
   A fifth person, an in
left, his spirit bleeding, i
to have my own ego shatt
   I do not by this descri
challenge their place in
personalities whose mas
their equally massive sel
a doctrine of indispensa
extension of leadership
to the creative growth of
   In the hundred and te
to have been elected pre
half of my predecessors
the early days of the org
the pattern of perpetual
as head of this, the larg
world, I know how my
like to believe were sinc
remain in my post as pres
   I did not. I quit. Not

as well as to the history that made us what we are. It must reject the encrusted and the outmoded tradition—the ways of mere habit that try, unbecomingly, to don the robes of tradition.

In my lifetime, Jewish leadership has had to grapple with cataclysmic change. There was the advent of Nazism and the embittering discovery that few Jewish leaders here or abroad fully grasped the enormity of the disaster that it projected. We may not have stayed Hitler's madness—a world coalition was needed to strike it down—but we might have marshalled greater resources and done much, much more in terms of human rescue.

On a happier note, when Ben-Gurion, flanked by the ministers of a provisional government, announced the establishment of Israeli statehood, the whole texture of Jewish life in America was affected by a revolutionary change; and we were not much more prepared, although we did rush to make up—and make amends —for lost time. The ways of yesterday no longer applied; they were out of date or had to be magnified to such proportions as to constitute a new frontier. Jewish leaders who had dragged their heels for or against the concept of a restored Jewish national homeland were forced to abandon their shuffling pace or, once and for all, forfeit their claims to leadership.

Whatever one's philosophical outlook on the emergence of Israel as a state with a Jewish majority, to have ignored its impact on the American Jewish community could only mean a mulish acceptance of blindfolds as an improvement in vision—a total rejection of reality. When spokesmen for organized anti-Zionism, dismayed at the massive transformation in sentiment that had taken place, tried to exorcise the apparition by wishful fantasies they fell out of step with history. Certainly there is room in Jewish life for a legitimate anti-Zionist leadership. But what pretends to that role today seems to me an incantation in monotone, mesmerized, meaningless where it is not damaging.

The Hitler era and the rebirth of Israel, extremes in Jewish experience, are vivid illustrations that Jewish life does not stand still. Less dramatic developments in day-to-day Jewish existence tell the same story. It is both a task and a test of Jewish leadership to be alertly sensitive to these changes.

There is, too, a voluble element in Jewish leadership that is intellectually alive to what is going on and that yet denies its demonstrated vitality. Afflicted with a sense of doom, it exhausts itself in gloomy assessments that Jewish life is disintegrating and that its demise is foreseeable.

This is not an innovation of our times. It is part of an ageless echo of imminent doom. The persistence of our people has been matched, in unbroken tradition, by the persistence of those forever scanning the horoscope and forecasting an end to Jewish continuity. From the angry prophets of Biblical Judaism to the pessimists of our own generation, Jewish life has had its Cassandras who saw only the collapse and not the reconstruction; the disaster, not the rebirth.

These despairing minds, genuinely concerned with the future of Judaism, cast accusing glances at the new temples in suburbia, at the fund-raising banquets, at the sisterhoods' theater parties— at the many material evidences of a secular-framed Judaism— and dismiss it as lacking any spiritual meaning and as unsuitable for Jewish survival.

They may be right. But their impatience is unjustified and their rancor misdirected. They scold the community—the people and their institutions. Their energies might better be focused on an evolving Jewish life that has the capacity for sturdy growth. Only a leadership inspired by optimism, and as patient with people as it must be dissatisfied with the status quo, will do this.

A leadership that sees only disaster on the horizon will act by its depressed vision and rationalize what it does in gloomy terms. Such a leadership we can do without. If we believe there is a happy destiny for Jewish life in America we ought to choose a leadership that believes it too.

How we can evoke a Jewish leadership that will be conscious of and responsive to Jewish values is itself a problem. The leadership of every generation is colored by its own life experiences. Mine, tragically, went through an unchartered transition from the immigrant culture of its fathers to something new and still inchoate, having first largely depleted itself of Jewish knowledge and intuition. The pendulum is now moving the other way in search of a Jewishness intrinsic to our free environment. But this is not the work of a day.

There are, too, obstacles of pedantry along with the impulse to act by instinct and out of superficial sentiment rather than out of experience.

There are also signs of progress. I see it—and here I challenge the cynics—in the conduct of much of our philanthropy. There are glimmers of it in other areas of Jewish enterprise. The crucial need is to have it permeate every act of Jewish leadership.

I don't observe *kashruth*. I state this as a fact, not a boast. I don't know how many American Jews do. Therefore, *shechita*—the ritual slaughter of animals—has little direct meaning for many Jews. When it became an issue in Congress in the hotly-debated humane-slaughter bill—a piece of legislation that brought more mail to Congressmen than almost any other legislation then pending—I stood side by side with the Orthodox groups, a distinct minority. I did so on a simple premise: their hurt was mine; to enable them to live by their deep convictions was the Jewish thing to do.

My personal views on *kashruth* and *shechita* were of no consequence. What did count was the fact that a respectable segment of the Jewish community observed these doctrines as a matter of tradition and religious belief. To my mind, a Jewish point of view meant the preservation of an historic form of Jewishness, however alien it may be to my own way of expressing the affinity.

This leads me to what I think is another requirement of Jewish leadership. It needs to be guided by wide-angle vision. It must have perception enough to look beyond the inevitable, more limited local partisanships and consider them against the background of the total community. Commitments to a particular organization or to any one program must be modified or moderated by a broader responsibility. It is a function of leadership to relate the individual impulse to the total Jewish life.

This does not mean leaders who yield to every pressure. It does mean tempering partisan organizational loyalties. Its leadership cannot respond to Jewish life if it insulates itself from many of its aspects.

One encrusted form of Jewish leadership is gradually being dislodged: self-perpetuating hierarchies that were often imposed in the highest levels of Jewish influence.

It is hard to tell just where and how this Jewish oligarchy acquired its strength. No doubt a part was played by the submissive awe and subconscious caste deference of an immigrant generation before those whom they found here, settled with status, and with an advocate's skill in the English language. The condition was sustained by the ego-indulgence of some who were reluctant to surrender or even to share their mantle of authority.

I recall a meeting many years ago in a suite at the Waldorf-Astoria attended by four of the foremost Jewish leaders of that era. Each was head of an important organization in Jewish life and each was perpetually in office. If the impression existed that these were proprietors rather than elected servants of community life, let us say it was a token of their impressive stature.

A fifth person, an innocent interloper, entered the suite. He left, his spirit bleeding, in ten minutes. "That's all the time it took to have my own ego shattered by theirs," he said afterward.

I do not by this description mean to diminish their eminence or challenge their place in history. They were strong and durable personalities whose massive achievements derived, in part, from their equally massive self-assurance. Out of design they lived by a doctrine of indispensability. Its effect was clear: to inhibit the extension of leadership participation and turnover that are vital to the creative growth of a community.

In the hundred and tenth year of its history I was the thirteenth to have been elected president of the B'nai B'rith. Since about half of my predecessors served minimal terms of a year or so in the early days of the organization, the others must have followed the pattern of perpetual leadership. After six years—two terms— as head of this, the largest voluntary Jewish organization in the world, I know how my own self-esteem was sweetened by what I like to believe were sincere proposals from the membership that I remain in my post as president.

I did not. I quit. Not out of boredom with my task—the experiences were challenging enough for a lifetime career. Nor out of a passion for self-sacrifice. But out of a firm conviction.

The presidency of a Jewish organization is, with rare exceptions, wholly voluntary. In the case of large organizations, whose lay leadership has not abdicated policy responsibility to a professional staff, the job is often grueling, travel-laden, and time-consuming. Along with placing a man—or a woman—at the head table in Jewish life, it can also overwhelm his family and business life. If a volunteer really works at it he will, over a number of years, become weary and set in his ways. He needs to be replaced. If he isn't tired he probably hasn't been working at it. He ought to be replaced.

There is the opposing view that we may be replacing good leadership with bad for the sake of change. This can happen. But the reverse can just as well happen. The departure of leadership can make way for fresh, new, and imaginative viewpoints. New blood in its leadership may chemically keep the community's arteries from hardening.

Nor do we have to put the "demobbed" leadership out to pasture. As one who has spent six years in an exciting post of Jewish leadership, and thirty years preparing for it, I cannot personally favor being completely discarded. There are, as there always will be, avenues of responsibility for those with precious experience, although retired from office. But important as is this use of experience, there still remains the greater task of stripping the community of its oligarchic incrustations, of spreading its responsibilities, and of encouraging steady mobility in office-holding.*

Another duty of voluntary leadership—often most easily neglected—is to prepare for an informal and experienced line of

---

* This advocacy of a revolving Jewish leadership does not include the other extreme in which skippers in rapid succession shuffle to and from the helm. There may be some logic to one-year presidents among sub-groups or local chapters of an organized structure. It is lost in the levels of responsibility where leadership needs to be sustained with a sensible period of continuity if it is to make any creative impact.

Nor are one-year presidents a defense against oligarchy. In major organizations, the unstable leadership inherent in short tenures solidifies oligarchy. It merely transfers authority into the hands of another type of, to me, indefensible communal oligarchy—the professional staff.

succession. Jewish life needs educated leadership; and this has as its corollary the fact that the best educative force is experience in leadership. We serve ourselves best by widening the opportunities for that experience.

Today the public stature of the American Jewish leader is less dominant and decisive than was that of his predecessor a generation ago. This has little to do with comparisons of competence or capability. Good or bad, a new drama-surrounded personality, the Israeli spokesman, is eclipsing the native leader in color and in dramatic public appeal.

Any experienced Jewish lecture chairman or fund-raiser knows from intimate experience that a rear-bench Knesset member is a bigger "draw" with an American Jewish audience than its own leading native lights (among whom there may even be a comparable Congressman). The still-radiant and hushful glamour of Israel invests the visitor with the aura of the prophet—even if he is one without honor on his home grounds. The continuing likelihood is that the conspicuous image of the Jewish political state (a sovereign among sovereigns) and its dominant personalities will remain. A generation ago, American Jewish leadership, representative of the strongest Jewish community in the world, was automatically accepted as spokesman for Jews, even in chancelleries where the issues of Jewish rights and a national homeland were viewed with patronizing contempt or even hostility.

This is now changed. Israel is for real. A Jewish people, a Jewish army, a Jewish government—these are identifiable realities that speak with a voice louder than theory, and that endow its leaders with a pre-eminent Jewish status.

This does not reduce the need for strong leadership among American Jewry nor ask less of it. The spectacular struggle for a Jewish state and the primacy it holds in world affairs will not forever—or even for long—be dominant in the *internal* developments of Jewish communities outside of Israel. They will, inevitably, make way for the proper indigenous efforts for a creative Jewish existence in our own native national surroundings. This calls for leadership with a special kind of courage and persistence. We won't get far without it.

### 3.

An index to the multiplying activities in Jewish life is the spiraling growth of its "civil service." The extraordinary demands for administrative skills and specialized talents to keep the mechanism of Jewish institutional life in operation have given stimulation to a new profession—the Jewish career man.

He comes in a vast assortment of job classifications—administrator, fund-raiser, sociologist, pamphleteer, youth worker, investigator, job counselor, lawyer, ghost writer, and, of course, educator and rabbi. (Note, however, that the rabbi who ministers to a congregation is rarely categorized as "a professional" and would be deeply offended by the term.)

He may have been trained in a seminary or had graduate study in group work and social service. As of now, the chances are that he learned his skills by on-the-job trial and error.

He has chosen a badly undermanned field, unlike any other and with peculiar demands of its own.

He has, as a rule, superior working conditions—at least, on paper. In reality, he is not limited by the thirty-five-hour week; he generally takes home a loaded briefcase; and, oh so often, he spends his evenings at meetings battling ennui in making speeches or hearing them.

He may be well paid. More often he is not. He works with and for the lay leadership. Theoretically this is an artistic arrangement in the glowing colors of a happy volunteer-professional partnership in community service. Human nature being what it is, we find more often the familiar stresses and strains of management-labor coexistence. He sticks to his task with some surge of sincere dedication (more than you will encounter in most fields), mostly because he likes what he is doing.

The Jewish community could not exist without him.

The Jewish civil service is shorthanded. Talented men are hard to come by. One reason for this is to be found in the lack of adequate facilities to educate them for careers that require special qualifications.

A nonsectarian settlement house can staff itself with group workers schooled generally in psychology and with related social studies and experiences. The Jewish community center, if it is to serve its purpose, must add the plus factor of a group worker who is schooled in Jewish affairs as well.

Some years ago, during a discussion of Dr. Oscar Janowsky's study of the Jewish center movement, the facetious question was asked: "We talk about center programs with Jewish content. Tell me, what is there Jewish about swimming?"

Nonsense? Maybe not. One may probe in vain for Jewish "content" in a plunge off the diving board. It may however loom large in the environment surrounding the diving board and the swimming pool. It was not so long ago that the staffs of some Jewish centers had workers who resented "decadent Jewishness" in youth programs. Against them were the Yeshiva-trained youth workers who were prepared to sacrifice everything that was not clearly labeled as of Jewish content.

Neither prevailed—or deserved to.

There is a relief possible for the shortage of Jewishly-oriented specialists but the community has as yet shied away from it. This would be the community's sponsorship of graduate schools with special curricula that stressed the plus factor for Jews in their community services. A school of Jewish social service was attempted some years ago. It expired from community inertia. It is time we revived the idea.

Nevertheless, there has not been a total vacuum. If the Jewish civil servant (the religious specialist excepted) is not a wholly indoctrinated Jew when his services begin, the associations of his workaday world mature his Jewishness far beyond the level of the members of the community, and even enrich it to a degree above that of the lay leadership that employs him. The imbalance between the layman and the professional often become visible, with, as a

consequence, the vexing tendency of volunteer leadership to surrender its responsibility and authority to the professionals "who
can do it better."

There are, on the record, some astonishing cases of self-puppetry
by Jewish lay leadership. Wherever this happens—rule by a Jewish
bureaucracy—all wholesome efforts toward leadership growth are
frozen into immobility. The professional is gently eased into the
character of an overlord and injustice is done to the essential purpose of a Jewish civil service.

It cannot be stressed enough that community leadership demands
a degree of detachment at the policy-making level—the ability to
look beyond the confines of a single organizational loyalty, out
upon the total needs and character of the community. There is no
reason for the professional to have less awareness of this than the
volunteer. But there are psychological factors against his practicing
it.

For the professional has an overriding bread-and-butter interest
in his own career. He makes his adjustment by projecting an almost singular loyalty to his own special, if narrow, assignment.
Unlike the volunteer leader who can sit in as uncommitted policy-
maker in a wide range of Jewish enterprises, some of them even
competitive in nature, and who can bring with him a broader
perspective, the professional is committed to his dominant loyalty
by his very employment. He cannot, if he is worth his salt, offer
to compromise with his assigned responsibilities. His very nature
as a career man deprives him of the essential of policy leadership—
freedom of choice.

For the professional is not inherently wiser or more judicious
than the volunteer. He may be better informed; yet the superior
technician is not, by his role, the sage. Even if he is able to overcome the handicap of his parochialism he still cannot supplant the
volunteer as the focal point of authority since, by definition, his
responsibility is to defend the self-interest of his employing institution. Voluntary leadership must remain an untrammeled exercise
in community service free from the self-interests, duties, and colorations of the restricted advocate.

The professional is a stabilizing force for maintaining continuity in Jewish affairs. He is a guide to wise community action and, if he is worth his keep, a prod to arouse its creative activity. But when he also occupies the driver's seat, subordinating volunteer leadership, he becomes the autocrat, removed as all autocrats are both from the true source of authority and from the moderating influences of criticism.

4.

In the composite of Jewish life each level of leadership complements, or constrains, the other. The leadership of a national organization, of a welfare fund, of a Talmud Torah, and of the neighborhood women's chapter are each a strip in a complex latticework. When the workmanship is faulty, the interlacings tend to weaken each other, and with that to undermine the whole structure of community life.

We need not bog down in a chicken-or-egg dilemma to strive for a mature community that can produce enlightened leadership —and the maturity that ripens in a community when it has enlightened leadership. Begin with a simple program to restore in every Jewish home the tradition of rendering the community some *clearly defined* measure of voluntary service—something beyond the accepted customs of contributions for philanthropy.

This is not a pie-in-the-sky expectation, for it involves no upheaval in the community's habits. It need only be stressed and made as universal as once was the habit of sending Jewish children to daily *cheder*.

It can become—we have the promotional skills for it—a convention characteristic of Jewish life. It is social convention, we are already told, that brings an overflow of Jews on Kol Nidre night who otherwise rarely see the inside of a synagogue. The same nostalgias can be invoked to attract all Jews into dramatic self-identity with Jewish community life.

It can be made as alluring as a precious ceremonial; a dramatic "do-something-for Jewishness" campaign as visible to the entire community as family worship at Kol Nidre services. Its enticing attraction for children as well as for parents can endow it with the element of enduring strength, the symbol of status in the family, among Jews, and in the larger community.

This is perhaps a secularist-tainted formula. It will not, of itself, yield the answers to all the complex problems of Jewish leadership and Jewish life. It has the virtue of inducing a greater number of Jews into the thick of Jewish life. If voluntary service in some form could become the mark of every Jew, its effect, over a generation, would be to enhance, beyond measure, the character, the performance, and the inspirational substance of Jewish life.

It would also help in part to answer the critical question: leadership for what ends and of whom? The large, unorganized mass of Jews that stands disinterestedly apart from the actions of the community and that takes no part in it persists as the profoundest challenge to Jewish leadership.

For whatever the qualities leadership needs there is one essential it cannot do without. A leader must have followers.

# (7)

## *America Is No Intellectual Motel*

These days, I don't know whether I'm a Zionist or not. The dilemma is semantics, not ideology. My convictions in the matter have been reasonably consistent since the day, about thirty years ago, when I surrendered my membership card in the American Zionist movement. But that was long before 1948, a date when some of the definitions of Zionism in the American idiom were abruptly wrenched from their moorings. There is now an abundance of rotating theories on the nature of post-statehood Zionism, what it is, where it leads to. As an exercise in semantics, it generally leads into a philosophical cul-de-sac.

Possibly my departure from organized Zionism has ceased to be a definitive gesture if, as Ben-Gurion tartly persists in repeating, the American Zionist movement itself has departed from the classic Zionist ideal of return to the homeland and has thereby "lost its soul and all its Zionist significance." In his appraisal of American Jewry, Ben-Gurion finds little to distinguish the Zionist from the non-Zionist. Both share the same brand of heady enthusiasm for Israel's future, both willingly exert and tax themselves in that hope in every direction—except one. Zionist or not, they won't leave America—their home. A Zionism without a return to Zion is, to Ben-Gurion, a synthetic, and threadbare at that. When, in these terms, he wryly concludes "I'm no Zionist!" it is a demonstration of his pique and frustration with American Zionists. He is blunt about it; he is also, it seems to me, irascibly logical.

The jousting between Ben-Gurion and the reluctant American Zionists is intellectual swordplay, swashbuckling in its rhetoric, yet flagging in its conclusions. Even if it were resolved on Ben-Gurion's terms, it would leave the vast majority of American Jews where they are.

Zionism in America did not exist as a rigidly static concept from the time of its mass arrival with the East European immigrant until its day of triumph in 1948. Its forms were intermittently reshaped and its characteristics were amended and modified by the stresses of history and the strainings of its explosive personalities. The changing disposition of American Jewish life, the transitional growth through three generations, left its mark on Zionist purpose. The moment of truth emerged almost simultaneously with the new-born state: American Jewry, now deeply and happily rooted, had imperceptibly converted its Zionism from a political doctrine to a romantic ideal. The guiding principle of migration to Zion, the heartbeat of the doctrine, was stilled by the hospitality of an American society that gave Jews the freedom to adapt; to be themselves. So it isn't only that we American Jews now reject *aliyah* for ourselves. We seem to make, as the Israeli caustically observes, a philosophy of it!

It is almost dogma for the American Zionist, examining his present posture with that of the non-Zionist sympathetic to Israel, to decide that the demarcating lines were washed away in the tide of Jewish statehood. "We're both Zionists now," he concludes. If the new Zionist rationale is to imply *aliyah* without meaning it positively, he is probably right. This definition might make of me a Zionist. The serious question is whether it makes an anachronism of the American Zionist movement.

It is no paradox in the American Jewish community that the non-Zionist group (whatever that term *now* means) outdistances the Zionist group in philanthropy, economic investments, and support for Israel, although perhaps in no greater proportion than their respective numerical strength. There are some who say that even the meager emigration from the United States to Israel comes largly from the nonaffiliated. But all of this is no more a paradox than the fact that for the past twelve years Israel has been settled largely by immigrants who never belonged to a Zionist movement or, for that matter, ever heard of Herzl or Pinsker.

Ben-Gurion's displeasure with the behavior of American Zionists is not an eccentric sentiment; it is shared by most Israelis, particularly by the sabras. Ben-Gurion's distinction is his penchant for saying it out loud. His language may sometimes agitate his more circumspect colleagues, but the pungent words delight Israel's youth. Yet when the Prime Minister suggests removing the scaffolding (Zionist organizations) because the building (the state) is completed he is not only indulging in a taunt; he is pinpointing the crisis in American Zionism. His purpose is understandable: to remove any favored intermediaries between Israel and sympathetic Jewish communities elsewhere. To him, a Zionist movement that does not accept as a sign of its covenant with Israel the commitment to live in Israel is an outmoded cure in search of a new disease.

The Zionists have yet to devise a convincing rebuttal that is based on a difference in basic principle rather than being like a thermostat turned to a higher *degree* of warmth for Israel. Where there is universal readiness among Jews to lend a helping hand to Israel, talk of "comparatives" is debasing, even meaningless.

Can American Zionism endure in this new world? Can it insure its survival by seeking solutions that, says historian Salo Baron, are "not previously offered either by Zionist literature or by the Zionist movement or yet by life itself"?

Notwithstanding the acute quality of Ben-Gurion's logic, it seems imprudent to regard the machinery of the Zionist movement as having outlived any future purpose. Zionism in Jewish consciousness did not lose its metaphysical meanings with the stroke of political independence. Nor has the spiritual glow of Zionism, beckoning the Jew to his traditions, lost its incandescence among the stay-put Jews of America. Curiously, it exudes a psychic harmony for his staying put. This because Zionism, historically, has meant so many different things to so many different Jews.

As from a rich fruit pudding, you could pick out this or that plum and hold it forth as *your* value in Zionism. If you were philanthropically minded you could select from the Zionist pudding those precious elements that held out the promise of resettlement in Zion for the displaced, homeless Jew. If you were culturally minded you could thrill to the promised renaissance of the Hebrew language and the re-emergence of Hebrew culture. If you were religious-minded you could see in Zionism the appealing poetical mystique of a reborn Jewish homeland.

Above all, Zionism for the deeply committed American Zionist became his sheltering umbrella; with it he withstood the hostile elements of a gentile world, protected by his faith from the harsh thrusts of anti-Semitism and insulated from the waywardness of the assimilating Jew. He could walk through the storms with his Jewish dignity intact. Jewish statehood was its guiding star, but Zionism as a way of life for many American Jews was accepted as an end in itself.

The future cadence of American Zionism may very likely honor the memory of Herzl while abandoning for itself most of his theories. After all, if you had been drawn to Zionism by its philanthropic aspirations, you are free to continue to help settle Jews in Israel without being a Zionist. A non-Zionist can join you in that impulse; so can a rational anti-Zionist. There is nothing to stop you; there is everything to induce you.

If you are culturally minded, again you need no restrictive label. Any Jew can derive satisfactions from a close relationship to an old Hebrew culture reborn into the twentieth century. For that matter, you don't need to be a Jew at all to respond to this appeal, any more than you have to become an Athenian in order to be drawn to classical Greek culture, or become an Italian in order to immerse yourself in Dante or Michelangelo.

What, then, remains of the distinction between the American Jew who continues to cling to the label of Zionist and the American Jew who does not? In essentials, nothing remains—save the habit of the label itself.

In place of past distinctions American Zionism may now seek the means and spirit for inculcating new dimensions in American Jewish life that concentrate on bringing the Jew here and the one in Israel in closer rapport, each committed to the permanency of Jewish traditions and ideals wherever Jews choose to live, each more intelligently aware of the other's design for living, each a partner in the quest for a meaningful Jewish unity. It may be a new and strange brand of Zionism or, as Ben-Gurion avers, no Zionism at all. By whatever name, however, it deals with reality. And just as the state is now real, so are the confusions of the Israeli and the American Jew about each other.

## 2.

Jewish communities outside Israel fall into three categories. There are those who live in poverty-stricken countries with deplorably low standards of living, with backward governments, and with, as a result, the same urges to try to better their lives by migrating elsewhere that impelled all those who emigrated to America—from the days of the *Mayflower* on to our own times. Many of these Jews, now economically or socially fettered in these lands, will continue to seek their way out, most likely to Israel. It is a general Jewish responsibility to help them resettle and reestablish their lives wherever their choice or opportunity may lead them.

A second group lives under forms of government oppressive not only of the Jewish identity but of all human dignity. The many Jews of the Soviet Union, for example, tenaciously clinging to their tradition through more than forty years of suppressive Communist acts and propaganda manipulations, are a tragic example. Their perseverance may yet lead to their escape or perhaps to authorized permission to emigrate—in what may prove flooding numbers—to freer lands, including Israel. This is always a prospect, and a challenge to Jewish responsibility. It is, even more so, a challenge to the entire free world.

The third category is those Jews who live where Jewish life is free to flourish—in North America, in Great Britain and Western Europe, in Latin America and elsewhere. These lands are not poor or economically backward. Their forms of government and social structures do not restrict Jews from being themselves. These Jews, four times as many as those now living in Israel, will continue to live where they feel themselves fully at home. They do not propose to tear up their roots for a new life in the State of Israel.

To pretend otherwise is folly. The Israelis—and this includes Ben-Gurion—are not blind to this. However reluctantly, and however often with bitter thrusts at its presumed materialistic motivations, they accept it.

A prevalent view among Israelis, however, is that American Jews are unwilling to surrender their comforts and security for the hardier, less certain quality of life in Israel. At times they say kindly that they understand; but they continue to find it hard to accept. They fail to see the American Jew's decision as one based on an optimism for his Jewish future in his own land—the United States. "Even the best of the Diaspora, and America is that, is a Jewish fool's paradise," the more strident voices have warned.

Their pessimism, unconscious or deliberately cultivated, has given an ugly coloration to the word "Diaspora." It is a perfectly good word when expressive of the historic Jewish dispersion. Its perpetuation, however, as a present term of self-exile of Jews, with ugly connotations of a second-class Jewishness, has set up a block to understanding. To speak of America as *galut,* either physical or spiritual, is nonsense. A mature and fruitful dialogue between Israeli and American Jews will be out of the question until the Israelis recognize that there is no substance to the presumption that the Jewish community in America is somehow inferior. American Jewish life must be judged by its people, their work and their devotions, not by geography.

Israel has a sovereign right to encourage immigration. The "law of return" is one of the great moral justifications for its statehood— and I have little patience with the fatuous voices that tremble in embarrassment because Israel has a law designed uniquely to favor and ease the way for Jewish immigration. Those who deprecate the law as "discriminatory *for* Jews" seemingly ignore the core of Zionism's struggle and the rationale that created Israel as a homeland for the remnants of a shattered, displaced people. Beyond this, Israel as a state has its own compelling reasons for its permissive legislation; for if, in Zionist theory, Jews needed a state, the present Israel reality is that the state needs Jews.

But it is false and mischievous for the Israeli to predict the disintegration of American Jewish life and to use that jeremiad as a lever with which to prod large-scale *aliyah*. Importuning calls for wholesale migration ignore, among other forces, the sobering reality that American Jewry is the backbone for much of Jewish possibilities outside Israel. At the same time, no graver crisis could come to Israel in the foreseeable years ahead than a hurt to Jewish life in America. An America in which Jews could not, as they now do, feel fully at home, would be part of a world in which there could be no safety for Israel. Jewish commonwealths, too, like Jewish diasporas, have come and gone!

This is the pathetic futility of those Israelis who raise the spectre of anti-Semitism as a spur to large-scale emigration from the United States. Israel's leadership, it must be said, disdains this tactic. Despite statements occasionally made for home consumption—and what political life is free from them?—the wiser Israeli leaders are aware of how deeply Jewish life is integrated into American society and how genuinely most American Jews treat anti-Semitism as an aberration, not a norm, of American behavior.

Not so, however, the Israelis you meet by chance, so many of whom identify Jewish prospects everywhere outside their state with the anti-Semitic crudities they had fled in Eastern Europe. More than once, in the *kibbutzim* of the Galilee and in Tel Aviv's outdoor cafés, they have earnestly reminded me that "it did happen in Germany—and was there a more integrated and stabilized

Jewry than the German one?" This equating of America with the German society, even of pre-Hitler days, with its historic racialism, its militarism, and its goose-stepping Prussianism, reveals how little they know of America. If their fears were really something more than superficial nonsense they would have barren grounds for optimism about Israel.

In his speech to the 1959 B'nai B'rith convention in Jerusalem, Ben-Gurion acknowledged that "what happened [to Jews] in Europe I am certain will never happen in America." He recognized in the American credo "a new relationship between differing groups that came together to create a civilization on the basis of complete human freedom, of the dignity of man, and of equality —at least legal equality."

Yet, the very character of these freedoms also led Ben-Gurion to question "whether the great center created in the last fifty years in the United States is absolutely safe in its *Jewish* future." He drew the analogy of *mitat n'shika*—the legend of Moses being called to his end not by the Angel of Death but by a kiss from God Himself. "In the past, in several countries, something has happened to Jews who enjoyed riches and good status," said Ben-Gurion. "They disappeared as Jews by *mitat n'shika.*"

That material strength and political freedom can be a kiss-of-death for American Jewry is, to say the least, a jarring theory. In actual fact our American history shows a more profound experience. The greater abundance of "riches and good status" American Jews have achieved in the past half-century has not been attended by any diminution of the substantive values of Jewish life. Of forms, maybe! The move has been in the opposite direction: the escapist from ghetto poverty who shed his Jewishness as alien when he fled the East Side is now the middle-class returnee, pillar of a native Jewish way of life that encourages respect for our tradition, is adjusted to his surroundings, and is reinforced by all the ethical imperatives of his pluralistic American society.

In the mind of the Israeli (and in the words of Ben-Gurion), the American Jew who wants to retain his Jewish identity must struggle for it between two worlds: the world of his faith and that of his

gentile neighbors. He therefore finds his Jewishness—or so the Israeli contends—in short gasps: in Sabbath prayers in the synagogue; in a remembrance of the festivals; in a Jewish organization
meeting. Elsewhere, he swims in the same stream of daily activity as
the non-Jew.

By contrast—to quote Ben-Gurion—the Jew in Israel is entire;
he is not split as a Jew and as a human being; his life is linked in
"a single, human Jewish world."

> In Israel everything is Jewish, just as everything is human. Here one
> can forget he is a Jew for everything around him is Jewish. The roads
> are paved by Jews, the trees are planted by Jews, the harbors are built
> by Jews, the mines are worked by Jews—even the crimes are commit-
> ted by Jews! . . . This is the fundamental difference between Jewish
> life in its own state and Jewish life in countries where Jews enjoy full
> equal rights.*

It is indeed a difference—but a difference in what? Do the social,
economic or philosophical differences which Ben-Gurion empha-
sizes have any real bearing on either group's potential to survive
Jewishly? Is it basic to my Jewish future, and that of my children's,
that the bus I ride be franchised by a Jewish company and operated
by a Jewish driver? That my coffee at lunch be served by a Jewish
waiter? (There is no escaping this world's interdependency which
requires that the coffee be planted and grown by *goyim* in Brazil.)
Is the crux of the matter Jews living in their own state? Or is it,
as I choose to believe, Jews, wherever they live, living in freedom?

After all, the Israelis too, no less than American Jews, must
make their adjustments in terms of their own clear national needs.
The Jewish prophetic tradition, for example, calls for beating the
swords into plowshares; the state makes its natural demands for
military security. The Jewish heritage calls for a completely sacred
Sabbath; the natural economic demands in communications, security and the other requirements of a national state impose their
inherent and acceptable restrictions on this aspiration. The adjustments in these, as in all the other realities of a practical national
life, are for the Israelis to make for themselves.

* Ben-Gurion in his address before the B'nai B'rith convention.

I find Ben-Gurion's premise that only in Israel can the Jew be "entire" a curious adaption in reverse of the dual loyalty shibboleth. No human being lives by a single loyalty; not in Israel, not in America. It is in the complex of his multiple loyalties that the life of a free Jew is complemented and made complete.

One might easily paraphrase Ben-Gurion by saying that "in the ghetto everything was Jewish, just as everything was human." Certainly the ghetto was a perpetuating force in Jewish survival. Yet the Israeli's abhorrence of ghetto life is fiercely mirrored in Ben-Gurion's simmering dismissal of 2,000 years of Diaspora as an era that languished with "Jewish interpretations on interpretations of past interpretations," while the spirit of Jewish creativity was corroded by *galut*. There is a suspicion that this smashing rejection of Diaspora life, despite its strong philosophical base, is more for political effect than historical cause. Few persons—I am not one of them—will accept the view that nothing new and nothing durable came out of a 2,000-year journey of Jewish history.

On the other hand, and in company with Ben-Gurion, I find little in the ghetto that qualifies it as a sturdier organ for Jewish creativity than life in an emancipated world. It is precisely this faith in the strengthening values of freedom that distinguish the American Jew and the Israeli; not by their differences in social structure, but by the sameness with which they enjoy a free place in the sun. With all the travail and adversity that are heaped on him, the Israeli tells you that his is a charmed life. He now has something he did not have in the Old Country—he has free and easy identity as a Jew. This is no mean achievement. But the Israeli must also fully understand—he does not yet—that the Jew in America has it too.

The American Jew is not marking time in an intellectual motel. Along with most of my coreligionists in America, I identify myself fully with the American nation of which I am a part and which allows for my many multiple—and nonconflicting—loyalties. That this sets me apart from the Israeli Jew is clear, just as his Israeli nationalism marks him and his life with a stamp that is not mine to bear.

This does not negate the warmth of my acceptance of Israel.

Rather, it tends to set such acceptance in a realistic framework. I realize that my personal relations to Israel go beyond those of the interested bystander; I am an involved one. But if I am unconvinced of the wisdom of Israel's socialist-oriented economy, I am equally unconvinced by the eagerness of those forces in American Jewry who, looking in from the outside, want to refashion that economy, or some other feature of Israeli life, to their own taste. This is not the role of the bystander, nor can he succeed at it.

Just as Israel today is not the Israel of May 14, 1948—so will the next generations of Israeli and American Jews experience fundamental changes. The links now forged out of sentiment and out of rapid reaction to crisis must be strengthened in the future in an enduring permanency and out of a creative and balanced reciprocity.

I do not expect complete identity of views between Israel's Jews and my native Jewish community. How can there be? Israel is a political entity with its own national problems and its own processes and pace of development. I do not expect the Israeli to share my outlook as an American Jew, at home in my native land. There may even be tensions and dissatisfactions between us. But throughout we have many purposes in common; and these can thrive only as the Israeli Jew understands my feelings and my optimism for my Jewish future here in the United States, just as I must understand his national policy decisions. He must learn to understand them because this, when you get right down to it, is how American Jews feel; this is where and how they choose to live. The Israeli may wish it otherwise; but if he is practical, he will come to terms with this anchor reality.

It is a significant truth that the re-emergence of the Jewish commonwealth has become a pervading fact for Jewish life in the free world. Every Jew, not omitting the confirmed anti-Zionist, is affected by and concerned with it. In the foreseeable years ahead, Israel will, I do not doubt, continue to have its impact, and much of what Jews undertake as Jews will be colored by what happens in that country.

But the quality of that concern will undergo its natural evolution. In due course the startling novelty of Israel, so easily dramatized and glorified these past years, will wear off. A generation of Jews now in its teens will have lived its life, whether in Israel or elsewhere, in the familiar acceptance of Israel's statehood. This, too, is an imminent, significant reality; and it will tend to reduce the sense of vicarious glory that has played, like a gypsy violin, on the emotions of our generation.

The transition from a recurrent crisis relationship, inescapable in the emergencies of Israel's formative years, to a long-term meaningful rapport, will call for something more substantial, if less thrilling, than starry-eyed emotionalism. This kind of reaction to the Israeli drama and its crises sequences has no permanent staying power; it can, in fact, become an abrasive when the crises are past. Farsighted Israelis speak with troubled prescience of American Jewry's outpouring of gift dollars for Israel. Nobody likes being indebted to and reliant on a rich uncle.

We speak of the "cultural bridges" and "creative alliances" still to come. But these are as yet only catch phrases. There are really no sound plans for "the bridges." Nor has there been much hard probing for the practical dimensions that can link, wholesomely, the Jews of America and the Jews of Israel. There cannot be any until some postulates are firmly agreed to.

The Israeli picture of the American Jews as sybaritic, as rootless, as living in a world of make-believe, must be rejected as the caricature that it is of our flourishing, potentially and actually, creative life.

The American Jew, in turn, must stop falsifying the Israeli by insisting that he pose in a posture of heroic infallibility. The Israeli may, for a while, strike and maintain that pose as a sop to sentiment. But he has long ago wearied of it—and is irritated by the request. He laughs at "our American worshipers who make us a vicarious outlet for their own Jewish shortcomings." He is human, not a divine incarnation. He wants to be seen with his human qualities, both virtues and defects.

I see the basic problem as one that must be met by the youth of both countries. Unlike those of my generation, they are growing up in a vastly different setting than that which shaped our awareness of and reactions to Israel. We lived in an unprecedented epoch of Jewish history. We have been actors in two overpowering dramas that stirred our Jewish consciousness deeply: the Nazi holocaust that erased six million of our people and, on its heels, the rebirth of Jewish statehood. But for succeeding generations, these will be events read about, not experienced. The shock and the sense of triumph will have receded into the impersonal annals of recorded history. The dramatic lights will be dimmed, making way for the normal shadings of normal days and nights.

### 3.

What will there be to commit the American teen-ager and his sabra counterpart to enterprise in common?

As a basis, we need to understand that the Jewish heritage, and Judaism itself, are not coefficients of the State of Israel. Far too many Israelis, and not a few American Jews, tend to equate Judaism and Israel as if the universal majesty of our prophetic heritage can have any confining political limits.

Many fail to see the danger that Israel nationalism may become a complete substitute for the fundamental bonds of our historic religious faith. They see only the American—not the Israeli—modifications of the Old World religious expression of Judaism. They need to see both. I do not question the Israeli's right to take religion on his own personal terms. But the Israeli who finds his whole satisfaction in the state itself can be a Baal worshiper, the betrayer of Judaism's universal calling.

The contentions of those who chide Israel either for its irreligious behavior or its theocracy are, to me, less important than the need for Israel's awareness that much of the future of Jewish life depends upon its perpetuation as a center of *Judaism*. Not alone for the Orthodox point of view, but for the other religious attitudes of the world's Jews. The harmonious interplay of a world-wide Jewish community is threatened when, in the sacred range of the Holy Land, one interpretation of Judaism denounces and anathematizes all others. I would not ask any Jew to alter his faith, nor challenge his way of expressing it. But I contend that for the understanding essential to a wholesome Jewish identity, a demonstrated respect for the various forms of contemporary Judaism is a prime requisite.

Just as sabras learn English, so can it become a matter of deep personal involvement for the American Jew to learn modern Hebrew. A generation or so hence—no doubt confounding the critics who have relegated American Jewish life to slow erosion—it may well be unfashionable for an educated American Jew to be without at least a nodding knowledge of Hebrew. Other cultural and spiritual bonds are possible at many levels. We find them now, sporadically. Herman Wouk sells well in the Jerusalem book stalls. The Israeli Philharmonic and the Inbal dancers are popular attractions when they tour the United States.

This cultural interplay, to some extent automatically generated by the very existence of a lively state, can be planned for with more encouraging expectations.

A deeper Jewish education here—above all, an education by service—will draw many into the active vortex of contemporary Jewish life. In the process, young Americans will understand the forces that are shaping the sabra's way of life. A parallel effort in Israel will enable the sabra, in turn, to acquire a more accurate image and a deeper understanding of the true character of our American Jewish life.

If the American Jew is not a candidate for emigration; he is nonetheless an eager, insatiable tourist. Transoceanic sailings and flights have a high proportion of Jews. His increasing interest in Israel can be depended on. It will grow, more and more expansively, with the present frenetic visitor to Israel, intoxicated by the novelty of Jewish nationhood, making way for the more normal and purposeful traveler, with solid interests in a social, religious, cultural, and economic exchange with the people and institutions of Israel.

We can also look forward to the day when economic developments will make it possible and essential for Israelis to visit America in greater numbers. More than once I have been amused and delighted by the transformed views of the sabra who has been visiting these shores. He arrives with strange notions, largely of sordid American Jewish fleshpots. He leaves—if he has stayed long enough—with a stunned astonishment at the momentum of American Jewish life and at the depths of its native expressions as well as of its feelings for Israel.

Emergencies aside—perhaps Jewish life would be starkly unfamiliar without them—we shall soon see Israel primarily concerned with its own hopefully self-reliant economic future. I leave it to the economists to forecast the day when Israel will cease to be a borrower and a "have not" nation. It may be some time off, but, given the ingenuity and determination of its people, the day will come. As a businessman familiar with balance sheets, I see the statistics of Israel's accelerating economy as harbingers and indices of a strong and self-reliant nation.

It will be a long pull until the books are balanced. For myself, I have a deep faith that the young Israeli leadership, when it succeeds the old-line leaders, will hasten that day. The old-timers came to power the hard way, through intense dedication, often to abstractions. They did what energy and even genius in organization alone could not. The stern realities of an emerging industrialized society were, at times, in conflict with and yielded to their *kibbutz* idealism. Many of the old-timers have been reluctant, for ideological and political reasons, to face up to the challenge of the disparity which, experts say, gives Israel a higher standard of living than its actual economy and rate of economic development warrant. The old-timers dealt with the problem not by an effort to solve it, but by trusting vaguely to a better, even a Messianic future. It is the rebellious voice of a young Moshe Dayan that pleads for "tightening our belts." And it is a voice typical of the younger generation's leadership.

The pattern of Israel's economic life is still subject to the variables of trial and error. Yet the time is approaching when there will be less stress on crisis "philanthropy" and more on standard commercial and industrial investment. To encourage this, American Jews will become aware that Israel, its self-respect, and its future strength, can best be buttressed through an economy stimulated by capital investments from abroad. I do not mean investments that are philanthropy in a different disguise. I do mean genuine *investments,* confident as I am of Israel's future and of Israel as an excellent business risk. For along with his special objective, the investor will dip into the greatest resource there is —the unquenchable spirit of a disciplined, creative, and dedicated people.

Out of these mutually understood and accepted normalities, the shape of a natural collaboration will emerge. And if Jews remain what they have been in history—people of vitality, of love of learning, of open-mindednesses to growth and change, of devotion to great ideals and divine ethical purposes—the inevitable processes will find infinite ways for their cooperative expression.

For, like the Israeli Jews, the American Jews too possess an unquenchable spirit of a disciplined, creative, and dedicated people.